C000039061

DR LAURA BISSELL is a writer, and mother. She has had her demic writing published in journals and anthologies. Laura is co-author of *Making Routes: Journeys in Performance 2010–2020* and co-editor of *Performance in a Pandemic*. Laura lives in Glasgow with her husband, daughter and two cats.

Bubbles

Reflections on Becoming Mother

LAURA BISSELL

Luath Press Limited

EDINBURGH

www.luath.co.uk

For my daughter Autumn, my mother Carolyn, my father
Bob, my sister Sarah and my husband Callum

First published 2021

ISBN: 978-1-910022-54-2

Printed and bound by Clays Ltd., Bungay

Typeset in 10.5 point Sabon by Lapiz

Contents

What are bubbles? My breath, pushed into liquid, suspended in air, blown by the wind, carried away until it meets a surface or object which punctures the fluid casing. Bubbles are a visual illustration of the way our atmosphere works; they show us liquid, air, gravity. But in their petroleum-sheened, spherical perfection, they also offer a lens through which to view the world, a rainbow-esque diffraction through which whatever is on the other side of them is visible, yet transformed. As my daughter and I blow bubbles every day I think about how extraordinary they are, how light and free, simple, yet complex. I too begin to whisper 'bubbles' with reverence as they float and glide upwards from our small square patch of garden, exceeding our boundaries and beginning to roam up and beyond towards the sky.

Bubbles, so harmless and childlike and fun, all of a sudden become beautiful bombs of my toxic breath, my germs encapsulated in a perfect sphere, drifting in the air ready to pop and spray my trapped exhaled air all over an innocent bystander. This is what the pandemic is doing, it is changing everything. Not changing the activity or the action itself but shifting the meaning of it to something darker, more dangerous and deadly. I hate it for this, for ruining these things.

Preface

'IS SHE OKAY? Does she look okay?' I asked my husband who was standing up, peering over the screen watching her tiny body emerging from mine.

'She looks great,' he said. Then grimly: 'You, however, are not looking too good'.

He mentioned later that he had seen my organs, my innards. Through the process of birthing our daughter he saw a part of me that I have not seen myself; he has *seen inside me*. Becoming mother has created this gory intimacy and allowed what was inside me to spill out and become visible.

In Rebecca Solnit's *The Faraway Nearby* she discusses the etymology of the word 'emergency'. Reflecting on her own relationship with her mother and the dementia she experienced at the end of her life, Solnit suggests that it is in emergencies that we are revealed. The root of the word is 'emerge' – to *appear* or to *be revealed*. My daughter's birth by caesarean section was the result of a series of decisions and deliberations which had to be taken in a short space of time and was therefore classed as an 'emergency c-section'. It was an 'emergency' in that my daughter very suddenly was revealed, emerging from my womb through a slice in my flesh to appear precipitously into the world. Writing later in *The Guardian*, Solnit suggests that it is in emergencies that we are exposed, 'as if you were ejected from the familiar and urgently need to reorient'.

Here, Solnit is writing explicitly about the coronavirus pandemic, a global health crisis which began in Wuhan, China at the start of 2020 and within the first months of the year had prompted a widespread lockdown and disrupted the daily lives of millions of humans around the world. This global emergency interrupted the writing of this book and is integral to my reflections on becoming a mother. The tone of my reflections change throughout; that is because I, and we, were changed by these events as they unfolded. This book is about two positive tests: the first at the start of 2018, a positive pregnancy test, which would set in motion my becoming mother; the second in December 2020, a positive test for COVID-19, passed on to me and my husband by our daughter after an outbreak of the virus at her nursery.

I am a white Scottish woman in my late 30s. I have worked in higher education for my whole career, in the field of performing arts, and I am also a writer and poet. I am a daughter, a sister, a niece, an aunt, a cousin, a wife and a friend. I am also now a mother. *Bubbles* is a meditation on motherhood and a memoir written in the process of experiencing the transition from non-mother to mother – becoming mother. By writing it while living it, my thoughts on motherhood are also *becoming*, unravelling like thread from a spool as the embroidering of the pattern is still in process. I can't see the full image that I am creating yet, I'm too close to the detail of the needlework, the labour of the small stitches I am working on each day. I'm aware of the way in which my seams are being complemented by the handiwork that my mother has done, and her mother before her. I know that my sister is working on her corner of the pattern and that both her and my daughter's efforts will be woven with mine to give a clearer sense of the overall tapestry. Or maybe it's not a tapestry, maybe it's a quilt, like so many that I have received from women to mark special occasions in my life. The fabric chosen with love and then pieced together over time, the care and labour of making it as much the gift as the object itself.

This book has been written in the presence of my daughter, in the small hours, typing into my phone while she sleeps next to me or gazes furtively into my eyes as she feeds from my breast. It has been written in the bleary morning hours before she wakes and in the evenings after she is asleep. I have typed it up on my computer while the white, ghostly shape of her head looms in the small screen of the video monitor which sits next to my laptop. The night vision on the camera makes her head look like it did on the ultrasound we had the day before she was born, a final urgent check on her position which revealed she had turned in the last week, or perhaps had been covertly upside down the whole time, we will never know. The surprise of finding out she was breech when I was eight days over my due date was my first real understanding of one of the greatest lessons of motherhood: that your child will do things you do not expect.

She was born in September and we named her Autumn. I've often wondered how she will feel about me writing this, how she will respond to me sharing these intimate moments of our first meeting and months together. I have worried that she will feel embarrassed or indignant about me writing about her in this way before she has the agency to tell me if it's okay. For this book is about her, it has to be. As I was becoming mother, she was becoming a person. An ex-student of mine from Iceland, now a friend, bought me a book to celebrate my daughter's birth: the aptly named *Autumn* by Norwegian writer Karl Ove Knausgård. It is framed as a letter to his unborn daughter and includes reflections on the world as he finds it: 'showing you the world, little one, makes my life worth living'. I hope my daughter will know that becoming a mother is one of the most significant facts of my life and I have tried to capture this before it is irrevocably lost. In reading this when she is older, she will know what it was like for me in this process of becoming, and as we forged our relationship as mother and daughter in those early days.

This memoir is about being a mother but also being mothered, being a daughter, and the ways in which new motherhood has brought my understanding of this into sharper focus. *Bubbles* has been informed by my experiences with my mother, a matter-of-fact Glaswegian woman who has been the single biggest female influence on my life. At the age of 30 she had just found out she was pregnant with me when her own mother died suddenly of a heart attack aged 56. My mother hadn't told her yet that she was pregnant so my grandmother never knew about me, the life that was to come. My mother (now in her late 60s) has solemnly told me many times over the years that she walked around with a towel round her neck for a week after her mother died to catch her tears. As a child I felt the loss of my mother's mother keenly, even though I had never known her. When I found out I was becoming a mother myself, I wanted to tell my mother immediately, should the same sudden loss inexplicably happen.

During pregnancy, I began to wear the pendant my mother had given to her own mother. It was round and silver, the size of a two pence piece with a ridge around the edge and the symbol of two fish intertwined in the middle. Pisces. We were all Pisces: my mother, her mother who I had never known, and me. On the back, word welts: *With Love.* Curving, looping, flowing letters scratched into the solid metal. I had treasured this pendant since I was young as a talisman of the women that had preceded me. Although my interest in astrology waned as I grew older, my affinity with water increased, and I would hold the silver pendant in my hands until the cold metal grew warm. I liked to feel the rough engraving under the pads of my fingertips. I had never seen my grandmother's handwriting and I knew that this curving hand was not it, but the hand of whoever had engraved it over 40 years ago. Nevertheless, I felt that this *was* her hand, that I could recognise the trace of my own mother's curving, left-handed loops in the shape of the cursive letters. My daughter breaks the chain of women in the family born under the sign of water but I will pass the necklace on to her nonetheless. I also pass on to her my surname as we gave her my family name (which I kept on getting married) rather than her father's, traces of both the matriarchal and patriarchal lines being woven into her story.

In these months of becoming mother, I often feel an oscillation between my roles and relationships. My daughter sees me as mother, but to my mother I am daughter. This feeling of being simultaneously adult and child occurs frequently when we are all together, all generations in the same room. I have missed this so much since the lockdowns began. I look at pictures of my mum when she is my age. We look the same.

Throughout my pregnancy and during the first year of her life I keep a journal for my daughter, moving between *her* and *you*, unsure at times of how to address her, trying to keep my handwriting neat enough to be comprehensible to her (to *you*) should she read these thoughts when she is older. I want her to know that she is loved, that the moments I am spending with her are important and intimate, that they are significant to me and I hope they will be for her. The question of how to live a meaningful life has been recontextualised through motherhood: what used to give my life worth no longer has the same power. What is it to live a meaningful life? Who and what gives it meaning? My life is inextricably bound with her life, our family a series of people knotted together by genetics and love.

This book has also been influenced by some literary 'mothers': writers I admire and look up to. Janice Galloway, Simone de Beauvoir, Jeanette Winterson, Rachel Cusk, Dani Shapiro, Ann Patchett, Kathleen Jamie, bell hooks, Rebecca Solnit, Zadie Smith (and others) all tell the stories of their lives through their writing. I never thought I would tell mine but now, as I read my daughter the children's versions of the life stories of feminist icons, I am showing her that these women's lives and the telling of their stories is important. How can I then insist mine is not? That ours is not? As Adrienne Rich asks in *Of Woman Born*, 'but what was it like for women?'

Bubbles attempts an impossible task: to describe or fix an experience that has been joyful, challenging and often contradictory, and that is ongoing. As I write, I am still becoming mother, as I imagine I will continue to do for the rest of my life. Rosi Braidotti argues that what sustains the process of becoming-subject is 'the will to know, the desire to say, the desire to speak'. As I become mother, I desire to speak of it, to say aloud what was whispered to me about motherhood, only when I was pregnant and had committed to the task. Rachel Cusk says in *A Life's Work*, that the experience of motherhood loses nearly everything in its translation to the outside world. I would ask that readers view this offering as *this* mother's attempt to know, to translate, to say and to speak what I have learned in these mother months.

CHAPTER 1

Burgeoning

AT 4.00AM ON the morning of 4 January I found out. I knew that the test was supposed to be most accurate if done first thing in the morning, but having obtained a negative pregnancy test result a few days before (Friday, the day of my friend's post-Christmas party), the blue cross when it appeared was a surprise. I must have been pregnant over Christmas and not known. A special Christmas present. My husband had been keen to be awake when I took the test so we could wait for the outcome together, but as it was so early in the morning (and as I was sure that I was not pregnant) I didn't wake him until my bleary eyes realised the magnitude of what the plastic stick was telling me. I ran through to the bedroom and pounced on him, my words coming out in a rush. 'I'm pregnant. It's positive. We are having a baby. We are having a baby.'

The day I found out I was pregnant I started handwriting a daily journal and endeavoured to write a poem for every day of my pregnancy alongside my diary entry. This was too ambitious and petered out after the first fortnight, but I kept my journal up devotedly throughout, documenting every single day of my pregnancy. Even when I was in hospital, I wrote up my birth experience in a torrent of writing, filling eight pages. I had not kept a journal since I was a teenager but had written them frequently from early childhood till around the age of 15. I slipped very easily back into this practice, 20 years later, like revisiting an old friend. I had often questioned in the interim who diaries were for and I remembered Virginia Woolf's diaries as her way of constructing the version of herself she wanted the world to see posthumously. I thought also of Sylvia Plath's diaries, first published as a massive tome in the 1990s. I had used the WH Smith voucher I received for the John Hume Prize for creative writing to buy this book when I was 16. This edition was more expensive than the value of the voucher and so I supplemented it with my own money from my Saturday job as a junior at a local hairdresser, where I would sweep hair, make coffees and shampoo the soft heads of elderly ladies who came in for their perms and blue rinses. Plath's diaries amazed me. I had read *The Bell Jar* and *Johnny Panic and the Bible of Dreams* and I knew of her history of depression and her suicide. But her diaries were the light, beautiful thoughts of a young, keen mind and I loved dipping in and out of them over the years, picking up at the page where my black cat bookmark indicated my last dalliance with her thoughts. I set some intentions in the journal I started the day I found out and which I wrote in every day for a full year after I learned I was pregnant. I continued to write after this but not every day, the demands of a new baby taking up more and more time as she was awake longer and required more stimulation and play.

I told my sister the day I found out. We knew we were supposed to wait until the 12-week scan to tell people because of the risk of miscarriage, but my sister has always been my closest confidante and I knew as soon as she saw me that she would see my secret in my face, so I drove round to her house and blurted it out. A few days later, she phoned in a panic to say she had shingles and was worried because we had hugged again and again when I had gone round to tell her the news. This was the first glimmer of anxiety around illness and health that I learned is such a big part of motherhood.

As an academic, my first response to finding out I was pregnant was to do what I always do: read a lot of books to try to understand it more fully. In my email *adieu* to the students, I jokingly referred to my absence being to my undertaking a new 'research project' into motherhood. Perhaps this was only half a joke, as I found myself reading, annotating and note-taking from Ina May and others as though I intended to write an article about the topic. I approached pregnancy as a reader, a researcher, an academic and a writer. My body, however, was not content with this cerebral approach and made its experiences, needs and developments very clear throughout. Being pregnant is the most aware I have ever been of my body. It is the time I have had to listen most keenly and relinquish most control to it. Even now I write as though it is something other, something I was up against, but actually it was the most kinship, affection and understanding I have felt for my physical self in my lifetime.

When my body needed sleep I slept, when it needed food I ate (what food it needed seemed to be largely baked potatoes with butter, salt and cheese, hearty, plain comfort food).

When it needed fluids I drank deeply and the thirst I experienced through pregnancy and breastfeeding was insatiable; I could not get enough fluids in my body, despite night-time guzzlings of orange juice out of the carton in the fridge on missions to quell my drouth. I missed events, coming home from work early to crawl up to bed into the oblivion of pregnancy sleep; I cancelled plans at the weekend so I could feed my addiction to slumber. I was a slave to the requests of my body and it made me wonder why I had so often ignored my body's needs, working late and then not sleeping, missing lunch so that I could fit in another meeting, filling my weekends up with things I felt obligated to do, then starting the week exhausted. My pregnancy was cause for reflection on these things and an acknowledgment of the need to recalibrate.

At a conference in Dartington when I was seven months pregnant, one of the participants came up afterwards to speak to me. I was researching the sea and performance and had cited the following passage from writer and sea historian Philip Hoare:

> In the womb we swim in salty water, sprouting residual fins and tails and rudimentary gills, turning in our little oceans, queer beasts that might yet become whales or fish or humans. We first sense the world through the fluid of our mother's belly; we hear through the sea inside her.

Donna, the woman who approached, asked if I intended on having a water birth as she had been struck by this quote. I told her that yes, I hoped to have a water birth and she intimated that both her daughters had been born in birthing pools. She confided that what you don't realise is that when you have a water birth, the water becomes murky as it mixes with your bodily fluids and that when the baby is born you have to move your hands around in the water until you find the baby to bring it up for its first breath of air. She told me that she had grasped in the water to find both of her children and was eager for me to understand that this was what I was going to have to do if I had a water birth. I would have to help my daughter transition from the sea inside me, via the birthing pool, to the world outside of my womb. This insider knowledge was passed on to me, like so many things in pregnancy and childbirth, as a warm intimation, a compassionate attempt to prepare me for the things that you don't know and that no one tells you.

Before I became a mother, some of the most hurtful things that have been said to me about my decision or otherwise to have children have come from other women. The choice to have children or not feels like a personal one and I am writing from the privileged perspective of someone who has not experienced struggles with infertility or pregnancy loss, like many people have. My own experience of questioning my childfree status had punctuated my existence since my late 20s. It seems at this age that the pressure to procreate ramps up and escalates further after your 30th birthday. Exacerbated by hysterical articles about how your fertility drops off a cliff after 35, my friends and I felt the uneasiness around these conversations as the years into our 30s notched up one by one. I gave birth when I was 35 and have no doubt that the fears pedalled around infertility for women in their late 30s influenced my decision on when to start trying for a baby. I remember thinking how I would hate to put it off for so long to then have issues with conceiving and regret it. An acquaintance of mine told me how a visit to her doctor at age 35 turned into a grilling about her intention to have children. When the (female) doctor asked if she was planning on starting a family, adding that if she was she should not hang about, my acquaintance blurted out 'Cherie Blair had a child at 45.' 'But not her first,' said the doctor, 'that was her fourth.'

When I was 30, a female academic asked me at a conference dinner: 'do you have children?' This question was not unprecedented or unexpected to me by then (although the male colleague I was presenting with was not asked). When I responded in the negative she pushed further: 'Are you planning on having children?' This kind of personal questioning becomes a common occurrence in the landscape of conversations with strangers and friends when you are a woman over the age of 30. Nobody knows if you are in the process of trying for children, if you are unable to have children, or if you have simply decided motherhood is not for you, but that these questions are permissible indicates the ways in which female bodies and the decisions women make around them are still up for public debate (often against the wishes of the woman herself). The second wave feminist agenda to claim control over women's bodies used the rhetoric of choice to campaign for abortion rights and access to contraception. This right to choose has been commandeered and repurposed for other agendas since, but the fact that women are still denied a choice in terms of speaking about the decisions that they make about their lives is evident in the way in which these highly personal, intimate and vulnerable aspects of identity are carelessly thrown about in conversation. What gives you the right to ask me if I intend on having children? How do you judge me if I respond in the negative? What do you think of me if I say I am planning on but haven't got round to it/have been focusing on my career/haven't met the right person? How dare you make me feel like I have to make excuses for my own life and the choices I have made; or worse, for circumstances that have dictated a particular outcome completely beyond my control?

I am writing from the perspective of a woman who was able to get pregnant naturally and quickly after stopping contraception. I can only imagine the pain and heartache that these kinds of questions, so flippant and loaded, so naïve and nasty, cause those who are dealing with fertility issues. 'Mind your own business' was the tempting reply on my lips when pressed about my family situation in small talk pre-baby. Now that I am a mother, I have found the question 'Do you have children?' on the tip of my tongue to ask others a few times but have yet to utter it. Having become a mother, I now feel the urge to ask this question to hopefully connect with someone over the strange yet common state of parenthood. I would ask this question as an olive branch to see if this person has also undergone the trial by fire of newborn-ness and infant-rearing but I have yet to ask it to anyone as I remember how affronting and difficult this question could be to the childfree person I was for many years.

The morning I found out I was pregnant, I felt changed. I kept trying to work out what was different. Nothing really yet. But the new knowledge made me sense my heartbeat differently, I moved more softly. Feeling every muscle movement as I rolled over in bed, my eyes closing softly to try to feel this more, to feel my body more. Cat-like, I stretched, luxuriously, before a tremor of excitement tightened my body and I wrapped the duvet around me, tucking it between my legs.

I had worried it might feel like an invasion, a taking-over of my body, being a host to something other. But I realised that morning that this *was* me, she was part of me and that I had nothing to be frightened of. After a few moments of lying listening to my own breath and imagining another, I pulled my body up and walked to the bathroom, grabbing my towelling robe on the way. Feeling the cold floor under my feet, I stood over the bathroom sink, took a glass from the shelf, and drank deeply. I looked at my face in the mirror. Eyeliner from the previous day was smudged into a half-moon on my left upper eyelid and I had sleep encrusted in the corners of both eyes. With my pinkie, I gingerly wiped it away. My hair looked tousled, tied back but loose as it did every morning. I peered more closely into my own face, looking for clues. Moving back, I tried to look at my face objectively, tried to see it as the face of someone else, as if this might help with my analysis, but I could only look at it as mine; it was mine. Not a special face, but my face, both known and unknowable, familiar and uncanny.

I had felt like that my whole life, that I was not able to really *see* myself. In photos of childhood, I looked like a different person in each one. 'Who is that?' I would ask my mum as we looked through shoeboxes of old photos. The ones from the 1970s of her and my dad all had a brownish shade and were matte in texture, the ones from the '80s looked cheap somehow, and the glossy '90s photos were larger, more garish both in their aesthetic and in terms of the images themselves. The odd black-and-white interloper was in there too; my parents when they were younger, my dad wearing cut-off denim shorts with long hair and a beard, eyes closed. They were closed in every photo, his head tilted, giving him a perpetually dreamy air. One of my mum in Brazil, her hair waist-length, ironed poker flat, wearing hot pants and a white sleeveless blouse, legs long and stance defiant, a palm tree and white villa in the background.

As we moved through the box of fragments of their lives, I would ask, 'Who is that?' '*You*!' my mum would say. '*That is you.*' When you were one, when you were five, when you were in the Brownies, when you were in that dance class, when we visited my bridesmaid (your namesake), on an English beach when the sun shone and you made sandcastles.

Each face staring back was a different stranger. A different face-shape. Different eyes and mouth. In some photos my hair was white, in others it looked mousy brown or dark. In some I wore dungarees and a stripy jumper and in others I had on fancy frocks and sparkly hair clips. Who is that? I thought. I scanned each image as my mum flicked through, looking for clues, occasionally resting my hand on hers as a signal to pause.

I placed my hand on my mum's thumb. Stop there. The photo was of a toddler, around two, sitting in a sandpit wearing a t-shirt that said Eastminster Day Camp. The sandpit looked to be in a glade in a forest and there was bright dappled light coming through the canopy of green leaves. The girl is sitting side on, a bucket and spade discarded in the sand. Her neck is twisted round and her face is looking directly into the camera. Her eyes look accusingly into the lens, her small mouth turned down and a green baseball cap, slightly too big, tilted back so the lettering on it is obscured apart from the word Camp.

As I looked at this image I remembered that day. The light, the sandpit, the clearing in the impossibly tall trees. I knew I was somewhere frighteningly different; I was too small to know I was not on the West Coast of Scotland, but in another country entirely, America. I was too young to know these facts, but I remember the feeling of difference, unease, foreignness. My body memory could feel the sand; soft sand, dry and light, the futility of my spade as I tried to make castles in the dust. A sound, a wailing, is coming from my face, my mouth mutated into an O. They are laughing at me, my language not fully formed, tentative. I had been confident with what I knew. The older children had mocked my accent, the words coming out of my mouth sounding alien, wee and impossibly naïve.

Did I remember this? Or had I just seen this photo more frequently than some of the others? Did I just remember my mother telling me about the day camp, how I had loved it at first and then, in the sandpit, had had a crisis of confidence. She would sing to me the Alan Sherman song from the 1960s, 'Hello Muddah, Hello Faddah', as an ongoing joke about my bad day at camp.

I always felt on the periphery of things and when I looked through those childhood photos I often felt as though I couldn't really see myself. Frequently photographed from the back or the side, half profiles or hair-covered fragments were often all that were visible. My childish shyness could be seen through the near-misses, glimpses and shards of myself in the photos. As an adult, I would peer at them, looking for clues. Who are you? And how did you become me?

I could feel it moving inside me. What a strange feeling to be a host to another living being, for it to be moving independently inside my own body. It was a sense of knowing myself better than ever and not knowing myself at all. When the scans had revealed the level of activity, skeleton stark against the deep black of space, of the foetus moving, twisting around, legs above head, head above legs, I had been shocked. All of this movement, all of this life! I had some questions I didn't ask the midwife as I didn't want to sound stupid. Does the baby have times of sleep and waking? When does it become conscious? Is it asleep the whole time, moving in a dream-sleep? Or is it existing like frogspawn or fish eggs, incubating, growing and floating in the amniotic sac? What does it feel like in there? When I had been late to our appointment for our first scan and had run all the way from the waste ground across the street masquerading as a car park to arrive ten minutes late, and had lain on the table, breathless and sweaty, the life inside me was agitated, jumping, rolling, on its front, hands to face, twisting. That it felt what I felt should have come as no surprise, but it did. It came as a shock to think of it as having agency already.

'This one is going to be a handful!' the midwife said jokingly as she struggled to get a clear image of the baby on the ultrasound. 'Is it?' I thought. 'Who will it be? When will I know who this person is inside me? When they are born? When they open their eyes, when they first talk, when they first defy me, when they first leave me?' The mystery of the life inside me.

In April, when I was 17 weeks pregnant, we took a trip to Italy. Three years earlier we had travelled to Oslo then taken a tour of Scandinavia by train – to the fjords of Flåm, Stockholm, Malmö, before flying out of Copenhagen. It was one of our favourite holidays and on 1 January, three days before we found out I was pregnant, we booked to go to Italy. We would do the same thing, fly to one city, Bologna, and travel by train to various places before flying out of Pisa at the end of our trip. When we realised that we were having a baby we knew it would be a different kind of holiday. Our trips usually consisted of exploring cities, museums and gardens before enjoying cocktails in the sun and wine with dinner. This excursion would prove to have more naps, less wine and a slower pace than our previous travels.

In Florence I read EM Forster's *A Room With a View*, which is partly set in the city. Lucy Honeychurch's observations about the tourists at the opening of the novel remain true today, as the city was saturated with American tourists. The church of Santa Croce is the scene for part of the novel, where Lucy gazes at the Giotto's and compares it to a draughty barn. The novel was written in 1908 and in 1966 the River Arno flooded, causing severe damage to the building. There were terrifyingly high water marks throughout the building and I imagined the stone floor I was standing on submerged underwater. We travelled to Pisa for our last stop. The rain was torrential and we sat in a restaurant that my husband described as being like a garden centre in Lanarkshire. On our last day in Italy, I stumbled near the leaning tower of Pisa. I had my phone in my hand, looking up a place to eat later and it broke my fall, cracking its screen off the pavement.

When I was six months pregnant I broke my phone again and lost all of my pregnancy photos from the second month onwards. The weekend prior, I had been keen to back up my photos, one of those jobs to be done that often loses priority to other tasks. When my phone stopped working and it became clear the photos were lost, I couldn't believe that I had not made backing up my phone the most important task of them all. Some vague fear about having my iCloud hacked and my photos stolen had meant I had never turned on the iCloud, so the images had truly vanished into the digital ether. I felt this loss of the documenting of my pregnancy so far as a grief. I had stood weekly in front of a small chalk-board hanging on the kitchen wall, my belly growing as I marked the mounting number of weeks on the board. I dreaded the question from my daughter: 'Why are there no photos of you when you are pregnant, Mummy?' I had fallen at the first hurdle of documenting her life before she was even born.

During pregnancy, a strange phenomenon occurred that I had never heard of before. As well as my belly swelling with the growing life inside me, a dark line, like a shadow at the bottom of a gorge, appeared from my breasts to my navel. This line, known as the linea nigra, is common during gestation and for me it lasted throughout my pregnancy and for a year after I gave birth. The mark was so distinct, so dark and strange to my body, the sharp line turning into a deep black well at my belly button, like a crater on the moon; it was the belly of another, not recognisable as mine.

In July 2018, when I was seven months pregnant, I had to travel to London to undertake external examining of a degree programme. I looked forward to the journey down by train, a solo night in a hotel and then working elsewhere for a day. As I was so pregnant, my mum suggested that she come with me to accompany me and support me with the travel. The idea of sharing the journey was welcome and I booked us tickets on the Virgin train from Glasgow Central. I met her off the train from Gourock and we bought sandwiches and snacks from Marks & Spencer before embarking.

We travelled to Euston then took a tube and another train to Sidcup. We had dinner near the hotel; everywhere was mobbed. We found a bistro and had a salad, posh macaroni cheese (my mum's favourite) and she had a glass of wine (while I, in my pregnant state, abstained). As we are a tight-knit family, it is rare that my mum and I have time like this, alone, without my dad, or sister, or both. We talked about her family, her childhood; she spoke about her mother and how she felt about her and how that shaped her approach to motherhood. She wanted to be affectionate and demonstrative in her loving of us (which she was) but I had not realised that it had been a conscious choice to counter her own experience of being mothered.

The day I was working could not have been entertaining for my mum, who stayed in our hotel room until check-out, wandered up and down the tiny high street, bought us food for our journey back and then sat in the park. She got to the station early in case I made the earlier train. One effect of pregnancy is that at the start of the day, your legs look almost normal and there is a curvature in the calf tapering to the more slender ankle. By the end of the day, all of the fluid in the body seems to fall victim to the forces of gravity and the calf and ankle become a solid mass resembling a tree trunk. After a clammy day in a board room I huffed and puffed my elephant legs as fast as I could to Sidcup station just in time to see the train pull away and my mum turn towards me. That was the beginning of an almost-making it, not-quite, slight-delay pattern that the journey home started to take.

Once we were on the Euston to Glasgow train we were able to relax, and while the bodies on the train, densely packed leaving London but gradually dissipating as we moved north, vanished, we had a whole table to ourselves and began to talk. I had some questions for my mother that I wanted to ask and I wanted to record her answers. While this made the conversation slightly stilted and awkward at first, we soon got into a flow as the rhythm of the train sped us towards home. My questions were about her experiences of being a mother and of being mothered. When we had spoken the night before in the restaurant, I felt we were having the conversation I had wanted us to have and capture, but this evening, almost alone in the train carriage as we crossed the border from England to Scotland, I was able to hear more about this, and also about how she was feeling about her daughter becoming a mother (and herself becoming a grandmother).

One of the things she spoke of most was not about being my mother, but about being mother to my sister when she had meningitis at nine months old. The words she used made me realise how much this experience had marked her, how much the potential loss of my sister as a baby had impacted her understanding and experience of motherhood. Yes, it is joy and love and closeness and soft warmth, but it is also terror, fear, the unknown, the unimaginable. The contradictions of motherhood were not known to me then, but I could hear them in my mother's voice, her words, and see it in her face as she spoke.

I did not listen to the recording until exactly a year later. The thing I am most struck by when I play it back is her voice. There is the noise of the train in the background, an interruption of the tannoy announcing our arrival at Motherwell and other ambient sounds. Over this, her voice is unique, her laugh and intonation only hers. It is Scottish, intimate, warm. It is my mother's voice.

I remember as a child the songs my mother used to sing for me: 'You Are My Sunshine', 'Scarlet Ribbons', 'Papa's Gonna Buy You a Mocking Bird', 'Little White Bull'. These were songs from her own childhood that she would sing to me every night before I went to sleep. The first time my mother was ill, I desperately wanted to ask her to record her singing 'You Are My Sunshine' so that I would always have this. I have always thought that she had the most beautiful voice, even although she is very self-deprecating of her talents. These are the songs I sing to my daughter now, and that she has begun to sing too. At a year old she would lie in her cot and say 'why'. It took me a while to realise that this was her asking for a song. I am not sure why she said why, but I would always respond with a lullaby, my eyes closed in the dark as I tried to make it sound like my mother's songs to me.

At eight and a half months pregnant I made a collaborative piece of work for a tidal island near Edinburgh. When I began the project in April with my friend and collaborator Tim Cooper, a sound artist, I was a little bit pregnant. By the time we shared the work in August, I was very pregnant. Going to the tidal island five times over these months to make the work became a good marker for me of how my body was changing. In the spring the mile-long walkway, only visible when the tide is out, was no problem and I was able to explore the island freely with no limitations (although I was always taking care). With each visit the walking became harder as my pelvis bore the weight of my child. Navigating the tidal sands, which had been enjoyable, became like walking through quicksand. My swollen feet, stuffed into hiking boots, felt like lead weights.

At the sharing in August, our final visit, I was huge. As I gingerly manoeuvred down the cliff-face, my back hugging the stone, belly bulging out, two tourists looked on in amazement. My husband was incredulous as to what I had been doing here over the past four months and I had to admit that I had not fully comprehended the physical changes that would happen to my body.

My due date was a Wednesday. Nothing happened. That night, I awoke at 2.00am with an incredible pain in my solar plexus. I woke my husband, remembering the early morning nine months before when I had shaken him awake with the same urgency. 'It's starting,' I said. He went into work at the crack of dawn to put everything into place for his absence. We had a midwife appointment in the morning and sat with the other heavily pregnant women in the waiting room. Things were moving, it had started, she was coming.

Two midwives examined me, beaming as I told them what I had felt in the night and the pains that were coming and going. The more senior midwife put her hands on my bump and said, 'Yes, she is looking good.' She felt my pelvis. 'Yes, on her way!' The student midwife did the same examination and they agreed. She was coming. They offered a sweep (a procedure to encourage onset of labour) but as things were already moving there seemed no need (also, I didn't fancy the idea of a sweep, from what I had read). 'Good luck!' they called as we left. This time I was beaming: my last appointment, I thought, until she is here.

Then everything ground to a halt. The pains seemed to be getting further away and less frequent. Around teatime I was feeling normal again. I knew this could happen, that early labour could take a long time, so I was not too concerned. But when everything stopped completely, I started to feel frustrated. A full week went by, no further contractions. I could still feel her moving inside me. What had been light flutters of movement months ago were now seismic shifts. She moved like an ocean-liner, huge waves lifting and stretching my stomach with each movement.

As I look back to these final days of my pregnancy, some things I did seem unfathomable. Going for a job interview five days after my due date, waddling in with a change of clothes in my bag in case my waters broke when I was doing my presentation for the panel. A week past my due date, my aunt came to give me acupuncture to try to get things going. I lay on my side on my bed as light streamed in the window and I could feel my baby moving, being moved, by the needles my aunt was manipulating in the base of my spine. I cooked and cooked and cooked until the freezer was full, preparing for the vast unknown of the days after her birth. I read and wrote and attempted to draw and spoke to friends. I waited for my baby to arrive.

When I was eight days overdue we waited a long time for our midwife appointment in the morning. It was the longest we had waited. Every woman in the room was heavily pregnant. By this point I had decided to have a sweep and when we were finally taken I consented to have her put her hands inside me to sweep my cervix. Patricia, the midwife, looked concerned. 'I can't feel the head,' she said then paused. 'I think she may be breech.' She explained that at this stage if the baby was the wrong way round then it was highly likely I would have to deliver by c-section. She stepped out of the room to phone the hospital to arrange for an ultrasound that afternoon and when my husband looked at me, he could tell how devastated I was by this news. 'It's not what I wanted,' I said. My husband said, 'I know, but we don't even know if she is the wrong way round. It might be fine.' He had to go into work so when he dropped me home I tried to do some botanical drawing to distract myself. He got held up at work so once again we were running to our ultrasound, my big belly bouncing as I ran. I was still hoping that the midwife had made a mistake and that the baby was the right way up, head engaged, as we had been told by two midwives the week prior. The ultrasound confirmed she was breech. When I saw her white head floating in the black fluid of my belly I felt joy at seeing her again, but also gutted that the natural birth I had my heart set on was moving further and further out of reach.

After the ultrasound we had to wait to see a consultant. She gave us three options: a vaginal breech birth (which they did not recommend due to a lack of expertise in this kind of delivery), an external cephalic version (ECV) procedure to try to turn the baby round (although we were warned this might not be successful as it is normally carried out at 37 weeks and may result in a c-section anyway), or a c-section. We talked it over – I didn't want there to be any risk to the baby but at the same time wanted to explore all possible ways of having a natural birth. We decided to try the ECV and the doctor said she would call at around 9.30 the following morning. My husband had to go to work so I sat at home alone. I phoned my parents, my aunt and my sister. My in-laws were on a flight to Romania and were not due back until Sunday. I wondered if they would miss the birth of their granddaughter.

CHAPTER 2

Birthing

WHEN I SKYPED Scarlet, my best friend in Australia, to tell her the news of my pregnancy, she said, 'I hate to steal your thunder...' and told me that she too was pregnant. Her original due date was the 20th and mine was the first of September. Hers was amended to the 14th and mine to the 12th. As both our due dates came and went, we spoke every day, both in limbo waiting for our babies while everyone else's lives went on as usual.

Scarlet and I had met in Sydney when I was there for my third year of undergraduate study in 2003. We had been performing in a student production of Frank Wedekind's *Franziska,* both as sex workers: in the production I sang and Scarlet got shot. We connected instantly and became close friends. What I was not aware of initially was how recently Scarlet had lost her mother, as it was only some time into our friendship that we spoke in depth about this. After my 18 months in Australia, Scarlet moved to Glasgow to study for a year. She returned to Australia, then came back to live in Glasgow for just under three years. She met her partner, who had also studied at the University of Glasgow, and they have been together since, moving back to Australia to live. We have seen each other sporadically over the years but remain close. I travelled over for her wedding in Sydney in 2013; my husband flew her over for our wedding, in secret, as a surprise for me in 2017. While in Australia for a conference in 2016, I had three days in Sydney and a heavily pregnant Scarlet met me at the airport to tell me she was in labour then proceeded to give birth to her daughter, labouring all through her own birthday to have her baby girl in the small hours of the next day. We spend most of our time in different hemispheres, as far away from each other as we could be, but it has ended up being at these pivotal, life-altering moments that we are in the same place at the same time.

The day we found out my daughter was breech, eight days over my due date, I video-called Scarlet, teary and distraught. She comforted me and said that she thought things were beginning to happen on her end. We wished each other luck and said we loved each other. I awoke early to a picture of her beaming next to her little boy. Her husband said in the text that she was hanging washing on the line in the morning then three hours later their son was born at 2.08pm. Otto.

I cried and messaged back saying how gorgeous they were and sending love. I went to my computer and finished some corrections for an article. I ran a bath and took a pack of frozen peas from the freezer. I had read online that you could turn breech babies by sitting in a warm bath with frozen peas on top of your bump. The baby was supposed to move away from the cold and down into the warmth of the bath, correcting the positioning for birth. The night before, I had repeatedly shone my iPhone torch from the top of my bump downwards. I had read that babies liked to follow the light and that breech babies could be turned this way. Looking down at my huge bump looming eerily in the white light under the bedclothes I felt no movement from the baby. I had hoped the peas might work and had also brought some clothes pegs to the bathroom as I had read that if you put the pegs on your pinkie toes, facing a particular way, it would activate an acupressure point which was also associated with breech babies and was supposed to assist in turning them. While sitting in the bath with my peas and my pegs, the phone rang. It was the hospital. 'Come in now.'

The hospital was calmer than our previous visit and we were seen quickly by a midwife called Joan who checked me into daycare and explained what would happen, and that Dr Gibson would be doing the ECV. She hooked up the baby and checked her heartbeat and movement. I lay in bed and listened to my hypnobirthing soundtrack as my friend who had had an ECV had advised, and tried to relax although my stomach was in knots. Dr Gibson came at 11.30am to do the procedure. I was glad it was in this ward in daycare and not elsewhere. I was worried I would become alarmed if I was in a surgical or emergency ward.

Joan explained everything as it was happening and put me in the breech tilt while Dr Gibson gave me the drug to soften my womb. I immediately started trembling and felt ill. My shaking became violent and my husband held my arm down to stop it as the doctor began manipulating my bump. She tried it in one direction and it seemed to nearly work but when she tried it in the opposite direction it was too much to bear.

The attempt to turn her in my womb that morning failed. It had been a long shot, but we were too far down the road and she would not budge. I was told it was 'unsuccessful' and as soon as these words had been uttered the doctor advised that we get prepped for surgery. She said I should go at 11.30 but as it was almost noon I thought she was referring to 11.30 at night: there was a moment of confusion where she confessed she didn't know the time but that I should get prepped for surgery now, it would be happening soon. Things were moving very quickly and at this point we realised we would be meeting our baby today.

They continued to monitor my bump after the ECV and the baby was fine. My husband went to get our overnight bag from the car and Joan helped me on with my sandals. I very nearly fell off the chair and as she helped me, I thanked her – her level of care and compassion had made the morning easier. She said that she had twins, Claire and Blythe, and as she said it I imagined our baby as a Blythe – a beautiful, breathy, Scottish name.

We were moved to theatre prep where we were seen by the nurse Rhiannon then each of the specialists, the anaesthetist, the surgeon and lots of midwives. They each explained their part in what would be happening while outlining the risks; the anaesthetist was the most frightening with the possibility (although rare) of paralysis. I had woken up that morning determined to have a positive birth experience whatever that might be, but as the doctor listed off the possible side effects and complications my mind wandered to other futures, other endings. I had never had surgery before and had to quickly try to mentally prepare for this turn of events.

Rachel, the surgeon, had described how the procedure might feel – 'like someone rummaging about in your handbag for keys' – and this is exactly what it did feel like, except that the handbag was my womb and the wet slurping noises indicated that it was not my keys that were being extracted. She said she was going to have to cut through my tattoo, a cover up of a tattoo I got when I was 15. My friend and I had sold our CDs before going to an ill-reputed tattoo studio in Clydebank. We got matching spiders, awful black spindly legs with a red spot on its back. A crude attempt at shadowing around it made for a confusing final image. I had been told by every tattoo artist I had showed it to that it was 'the worst tattoo they had ever seen'. It was lumpy with scar tissue and I finally got it covered by a large black design on my last day of living in Sydney, at a tattoo studio near Sydney Central called The Illustrated Man. For the 26-hour flight I had to sit with my jeans button and fly open, wincing every time the seatbelt grazed the new inky wound. The spider had transformed into a symbol which was now to be sliced open, each of these markings a trace of an experience of my life. I didn't care about my severed tattoo and laughed when Rachel confessed she had once had to decapitate a Winnie the Pooh when performing a c-section.

The staff kept informing us that we were being fitted in around other operations so we might not be taken for surgery until the evening, but then all of a sudden a nurse was handing me two gowns and it was happening. I had to leave my husband in the ward – his face pained with worry for the first time. When I entered the theatre I started to feel nervous and my breath and limbs began to shake, but as they talked me through everything I tried to relax and do my hypnobirthing breathing. The theatre was bright and full of bodies, chatting loudly and jovially. My memory of it now is very heightened: the lights, the loud voices talking about their dogs, everyone except me outfitted in blue. I told them I had cats and that my best friend had had her baby that day in Australia. I asked a lot of questions, curious about the process, what was happening and what I should be feeling. The anaesthetist kept checking if I was numb using a cold spray, checking if I could feel cold or a tickle, or nothing, until my whole lower half was sedated, my limbs asleep, no longer in my control. There is something filmic about the way I remember this, and some of the visual elements of the space return to me frequently, in technicolour. A tiny knitted hat poised on a stand in the corner of the room waiting for her head to fill it. One of the midwives had a Rhodesian puppy, she told a funny story about it. I told them about the tidal island performance I had done at eight and a half months pregnant. I was shaking but managed to breathe through the spinal (I was so worried I would start and the needle would slip and paralyse me – one of the potential outcomes of the operation that the surgeon had briefed me on previously). I lay with my arms outstretched, like Christ on the cross, as they swivelled the table from side to side to move the drug around my body. That gravity should be deployed in a way to circulate the anaesthetic seemed amusing. It was not frightening at this point, I just felt an intense curiosity as to what was happening. They did a 'surgical pause' where they checked over everything, before bringing in my husband: blue scrubs, worried face.

When he entered the operating theatre he looked younger than I remembered. They had erected a screen at the level of my chest which meant I could no longer see my lower body as well as not being able to feel it. At some point a catheter had been put in and I had the unsettling feeling that I was completely naked below the waist. I wanted to ask my husband if this was the case but didn't want to say it in front of the hospital staff. It was weeks after the surgery when I finally asked him and he reassured me that I had been covered by a sheet and was not, as I had suspected and feared, exposed.

I heard someone say, 'One foot out,' then my husband stood up so that he could watch our baby being born from over the screen. I could feel her head being strongly wrenched from inside me, the feeling of a vacuum, of the large bump that I had been carrying high (as she was breech her head was up near my heart, my ribcage) being removed was powerful. I felt her leaving me, I heard fluids splash, I listened for her cry, which finally came. The moments from her leaving my body and me seeing her for the first time felt so long. I will never forget the look she gave me when they brought her round the side of the curtain. Her eyes were wide open and she was glaring at me. I asked pointlessly 'Is that her?' They swaddled her and gave her to my husband as I strained my neck trying to see her from my supine position. I just wanted to touch her and have skin-to-skin contact but we had to wait while I was stitched up. He cuddled the baby and we chatted; a midwife offered to take a picture for us. We have these framed in her nursery – my husband looking impossibly young, holding her swaddled in an NHS blanket, me with my blue surgical cap on, beaming, with her propped up next to my face as they stitched me up out of shot. Her nose was covered with a red blotch, a birthmark one of the midwives said, but another said it might just be a bruise. It was bright red and angry looking. Before the surgery they had told me I was lucky having a c-section as her head would be perfectly round, and it was, a round head with round eyes open, alert, taking it all in.

Rachel, the surgeon, said she took longer stitching me up to make sure my tattoo matched where she had sliced into it (and joked it would cost me an extra £50). Eight sets of arms lifted me aloft then onto a bed as I was wheeled into recovery. I was elated, manically shouting, 'Thank you everyone, this has been AMAZING!' as they trundled my inert body out of the theatre.

She was finally placed into my arms and I fumbled with her fleshy newness as I tried to get her on to my breast. It was awkward as I had a cannula in my hand and lots of tubes coming out of me. Her body was red and wrinkly. After she had fed, my husband held her skin to skin while I had a cup of tea. The first feed seemed quick but when I looked at my notes the midwife had jotted it down as 30 minutes. This was the beginning of time losing all sense of meaning to me. I ate a whole bag of jelly babies that my friend Jenna had given me. I was so hungry after fasting since the morning that I didn't even notice I was consuming 'babies' until I had emptied the packet.

I had a strong sense that my daughter would be born at 2.08pm GMT. I had joked with Scarlet throughout our pregnancies about us labouring and giving birth at the same time on opposite sides of the world. While this did not happen and our birthing experiences were quite different, there was a sense of synchronicity that our children should be born on the same day. She was born at 3.21pm, not 2.08pm as I had anticipated, but Otto and Autumn will forever be connected, semantically through their similar sounding names and the fact they are birthday twins, as well as through their mothers' long-lasting friendship. My brother-in-law texted me the Earth Wind & Fire song 'September'. The first line refers to the date of her birth. I sent it to Scarlet saying that neither of us will ever forget that night, the first night with our brand-new babies. I had a sense of the Earth spinning on its axis; as Scarlet's day moved into night, my day was beginning, Autumn Scarlett's birthday – my beautiful friend her namesake.

When my parents arrived to meet her I was so high from the drugs that I couldn't stop talking. I can't even remember if she was awake when they arrived or if I fed her when they were visiting. I was glad they were there as my dad had sounded ill with worry when I called them earlier in the day. Mum brought a fork so I could eat the chicken and rice I had brought in a cool bag. They stayed till 8.00pm then my husband and I had an hour before he had to leave at 9.00pm. These hours immediately after her birth were hazy, I felt so elated but was clearly still out of it as I sent numerous text messages to people that I had no recollection of the next day. After he left, a nurse came to help me stand up for the first time. It was only then, the joyful hysteria of the birth abating, that I realised how weak I was and that I was bleeding a lot, in pain and that I was in for a long solitary night of trying to feed and care for my new daughter. This first night was very hard. Terror of the new responsibility and physical incapacity combined made for a long and traumatic night. I asked for advice from the midwives on duty, but I really needed someone else there to help me up and down with her. I listened to podcasts and tried to stay awake but she would only sleep with me holding her and I was so scared that I was going to fall asleep and drop her. When I put her in her cot she would cry. The woman who I was sharing a ward with was having issues with her baby too, so the whole night was disrupted as cries erupted from either her or my side of the room. Either the light was on and it was hard to sleep or the light was off and it was impossible to see to change a nappy. The first time I did it, her nappy was so messy with meconium that I used too much water and when I picked her up once the fresh nappy was on I realised I had soaked the mattress and her sleep suit. The midwife helped me put new sheets on her bed. I felt so useless. At around 5.00am I began to lose my grip on reality; I was exhausted. Tearily, I asked the midwives to help me settle her and they took her out into the hall with them. I instantly regretted this and wanted her near me so I asked them to bring her straight back. I felt I had betrayed her, that if she needed me in the night and I wasn't there she would never forgive me. I didn't want her out of my sight and felt the first strains of the bond that we would now have. This first strange, beautiful and awful night of companionship and getting to know my daughter is like nothing I had ever experienced before. I was in so much pain that by the end of the night I was delirious. I was counting the hours until my husband could come so he could help. As the light was coming up I had my hand in her cot, rocking her and holding her while trying to grab a few moments of sleep.

I had read numerous books on childbirth, attended antenatal classes and birthing yoga, written a detailed itinerary for the process of my labour – what to do in the early stages, what films to watch, music to listen to, people to phone (and in what order), snacks to prepare, what yogic positions to do. Having to have an emergency c-section felt as though I had swotted up for months then wasn't allowed to sit the test. I didn't have the water birth that I had planned, or the yogic birth, or the hypno-birthing experience for which I had been preparing. However, the idea of my womb as a little ocean, of the amniotic fluid that surrounded my baby for the nine gestational months as the sea inside me in which she swam, has provided me with much inspiration and comfort during my pregnancy and becoming a mother.

I found myself trying to understand the physical sensations of being close to a body that was once inside me but was now not my own. A small craft independent from the mothership, a tugboat now dangerously alone on the ocean but still tethered by a thin rope to my body. This constant state of movement, of flux feels like the most apt way to describe the changes to my body, life and sense of self that motherhood has brought about.

CHAPTER 3

Revelations

A DOCTOR INITIATED a paediatric check the morning after her birth, while I just about held myself together after a night of pain and exhaustion. My husband was not there; the paediatric check was at 9.00am and he was not permitted back into the ward till 11.00am. This designation of father as 'visitor' sat uncomfortably with me and I wished he was there to hold her and to pay attention to all of the medical information I was receiving in my bleary, blurry state. The doctor mentioned that one of her hips was clicking and that this could be an indicator of hip dysplasia. This is a condition that affects one in a thousand babies, mainly females and often babies who are breech. The ball and socket joint in the hip does not form fully or properly when in the womb and needs immediate treatment to ensure the bones form correctly when the baby is born. She said many babies are given an ultrasound for this at around six weeks but because our daughter's was quite prominent on the left side, we would get an appointment within two weeks. She said another specialist would see us later. When the specialist called, I missed part of the conversation but my husband seemed to think it was quite serious.

On the Wednesday two weeks after her birth, when we took her to the hospital for the ultrasound I was convinced (or had convinced myself) that we were simply getting her hip checked out. My husband said afterwards that the signs were there, the warning notes in the consultant's tone, the fast-tracking of her ultrasound. But I was oblivious, besotted with my baby, who looked so perfect and well. The hospital where I had given birth was the new superhospital built on the Govan side of the Clyde to replace the Queen Mother's hospital where I had been born. My mother always used to point this out on the train to me as we whizzed past Partick and Yorkhill heading into town to do our shopping. Elevated above the streets and trainline, its pink windows would sparkle with its reflections of sunlight and water. I could see its distinctive pink reflective glass windows above the skyline from the back windows in our house. 'You were born there,' my mum used to tell me and it felt good to be able to know where I was from, where I had arrived in this place.

The Queen Elizabeth University Hospital (formerly known as South Glasgow University Hospital before it was royally renamed a few months after opening) also had reflective panels around its superstructure, but while the Queen Mother's had that aesthetic block-ness associated with buildings constructed in the '50s and '60s, QEUH looked like a spaceship emerging from the streets of Govan and was nicknamed in local press as 'The Death Star'. It was huge and the reflective panels in orange and light and dark grey made it look like a hospital from the future (or an '80s imagining of what this might be). I had given birth in this hospital and thought it had seemed new, clean and efficient, the kind of facility you would hope to be able to be in when having your first baby.

Our return to this site this time was to the Royal Children's Hospital, next to the maternity ward. Its glass interior with a spacious atrium was welcoming and smart. We walked along the corridor to the x-ray department which was adorned with large images from Julia Donaldson books: *The Gruffalo, The Snail and the Whale, Stick Man*. We didn't know who these characters were, but we were soon to find out. Autumn had her ultrasound, a tiny wriggling mass on the adult white table while we each held a scrawny limb. Waiting in the atrium afterwards I was sure that she was fine, it was an anomaly, there were no external signs of any issues. The consultant took us into the ward and explained that she had hip dysplasia and would need treatment. Neither of her ball and socket joints had formed correctly. They were both too shallow, the 'socket' part of the ball and socket being insufficiently deep to hold the 'ball' of the hip joint. He said that the harness, a device that used straps across the shoulders and back to hold the legs bent and open, in an abducted position, like a frog, would be on for around 12 weeks and she would have fortnightly ultrasounds. If this was not successful in calibrating the hips, they would put her in a cast to hold her legs apart until she was four or five months, and if this was not successful then she would need an operation aged one. We listened, taking it all in, trying to process the right questions and responses. We wouldn't be able to bathe her at home, he said, she must wear the harness 24 hours a day and only have it removed by them at the hospital every Wednesday when she would come for a bath. Wednesday mornings in the Plaster Room would be her bath-time. Yes, we would come to the hospital every week and every second week she would have an ultrasound to monitor her progress. He had said this before and I realised I was asking questions he had already addressed. As if to move the conversation on, he brought out a plastic bag with a tiny contraption with straps and Velcro attachments. This was the Pavlik harness, the smallest one they had. It had a brown and pink pattern of ducks on the straps as if to try to make it seem more child-friendly and less surgical. I imagined that in the '50s this would be leather straps and metal buckles and when I looked this up later on the internet I was not far wrong. I nodded, taking it all in, yes, okay, this is the treatment, this is what needs to happen. He handed me a pamphlet on how to care for a child with a Pavlik harness and I opened it to images of smiling babies, their legs splayed like little frogs in the abducted position. 'She can't move from this?' I asked. 'No,' he said, 'she must stay like this all the time in order for the ball and socket to realign'. They only do ultrasounds and not x-rays at this stage as the bones are still forming, still shifting and malleable under the skin. I nodded. 'Okay. I understand.'

My husband squeezed my hand. 'When does the treatment start?' I asked. 'Shall we make another appointment on our way out?' The consultant was tearing open the plastic bag of the harness. 'It will start today,' he said. 'I will fit it now and adjust it correctly, then one of the nurses will show you how to change her nappy with it on, then we will see you next week for her bath and check-up.' I only heard half of what he said as I was reeling with the news that we would be leaving with her in the harness. As he was speaking he was fiddling with the contraption, examining it and opening it up to put it on. My hands were still, my breath shallow. 'Can you take her vest and nappy off please?' My husband sprang into action while I remained still. It took me a moment before I could assist, kissing her lightly on the head as I reached for her vest. Today, I kept thinking. It's happening today. He pulled the straps over her chest, the cross-section of the harness baggy across her back – even the smallest size was big for her as she was so tiny. A nurse was there suddenly, helping with the adjustments. When they had to reset the Velcro straps across her chest, the nurse covered my daughter's ear so she didn't get a fright from the noise of the Velcro. She lay docile, quiet, accepting. When she had the harness on, I could have wept. Although she was healthy and fine apart for this slight hip defect, it was hard not to think of her as ill or hurt due to the contraption. We struggled to pull her sleepsuit on over her legs. 'Probably need to avoid leggings,' the nurse said and indicated that sleepsuits a size up would be best. All her wee outfits, I thought, all her new clothes.

In the car on the way home I had a moment of devastation that due to the fact we had kept ourselves to ourselves in this first fortnight, to enjoy our new time together and my husband's paternity leave, now everybody would be meeting her for the first time like this, wearing this. It was a vain thought and I quickly chastised myself for it. I felt anxious about returning to the hospital every week, learning to care for her at home, not being able to bathe her and share the evening ritual of bath and bed that we had been conditioned to expect. In reality, our weekly trips to the hospital became an exercise in gratitude. Gratitude that she had something so treatable, something (hopefully) impermanent. There were a lot of very sick children in that hospital and our weekly trips to the Plaster Room not only became an enjoyable ritual of bathing her and playing with the water, but also made me think about how lucky we were. For them to have caught it so quickly, that it was treatable, that she was otherwise healthy, that she would hopefully not suffer any long-term effects from this early intervention.

On the way home, I phoned Scarlet in Australia. Despite only one in 1,000 babies having this condition, her daughter (whose birth I had been in Sydney for) had also had this, although it had not been spotted until she was nine weeks old. Scarlet was reassuring and positive and I felt that if her family had gone through this then we could too. Another friend also shared her experiences with her daughter's hip dysplasia. We had support and people to talk to.

Part of the enjoyment of Wednesday mornings at the hospital came from the attitude and support of the nurses. Instead of it being stressful or worrying, it became a playful ritual where the nurses would joke and laugh and speak to our daughter in a loving way as they cared for her. They would run us a bath then leave us to bathe her ourselves, returning to fit and adjust her harness, moving up in sizes as she grew. I kept her first harness, it is in her memory box, a slightly grubby straggly mass of Velcro and plastic straps. I will show her it when she is older, as well as the pictures of her as a little starfish, a triangle, a frog for the first three months of her life.

The thought of 12 weeks in the harness felt like a lifetime, three months of hospitals, additional care, explaining to people what was wrong with her when they asked (and they asked) – it was not how we imagined the first months with our baby would be. I wondered how a new mother who was on her own would manage this. Or a new mother who didn't drive or have someone to drive her to the hospital would manage to get to the appointments every week. I had imagined maternity leave as having a lot of free time and was shocked at how quickly the time was filled with appointments, health visitor drop-ins, doctor's visits and other health-related activities. It dawned on me as though I had been quite ignorant before: this is why you have the time off, I realised. It is a full-time job. My days were full (as were my nights).

And then, as though in the blink of an eye, it was over. The weeks that had felt like they were yawning cavernously ahead of us, each a barrier to overcome, all of a sudden were done. Her last ultrasound had looked good and it seemed as though she might have it removed before Christmas. 'Try not to get your hopes up,' I was warned by my parents and husband as they knew how deluded and then disappointed I had been about the initial appointment and the immediate start of her treatment. I looked back on that day feeling annoyed at myself. All I wanted was to take her home as she was, have time to process the news and then return to have the harness fitted. With the benefit of a few months' hindsight I felt so grateful at the speed at which it had all happened – of course she would have it fitted that day, of course the earlier the better. I could see all that now but at the time I had been blind, naïve.

The day she got it off, I had taken tartan leggings to the hospital so she could wear them home and a black and white t-shirt that said 'This Girl Rocks'. The harness was removed and we were told we could take her home. Just like that! We dressed her clumsily in her outfit – how easy it was to put a nappy on without a harness to navigate! How strange it was to see her in trousers! We secured her in her car seat – also different now she didn't have the harness on, we had to adjust it anew, then we were out of the hospital, we were free! We took a picture of that day, us all beaming, thumbs up to the camera as my daughter was held between us, her newly liberated legs dangling strangely below her body, adorned in tartan. Our routine of hospital visits and appointments stopped, she would have an x-ray at one year and then every year until she was school age to check that everything was still developing correctly. As quickly as we had adapted to our routine when she was two weeks old, we forgot it. We bathed her at home every night now. We dressed her in the pile of leggings that had sat neglected for all those months (we never did get through them all), and we felt so, so grateful for the care that she had received, that she would hopefully now lead a life where she was not physically impacted by this condition at birth.

How amazing the body is, I thought. How malleable and adaptable and accommodating. How marvellous that these contraptions exist, that she could have this treatment aged two weeks and for her body to fix itself.

When the harness was removed, just before her first Christmas, for months she still slept on her back with her legs splayed, spread-eagled as though she was still bound by the harness. Although it wasn't there anymore, she had learned to sleep this way, it was comfortable for her and so she would sleep, like a starfish on the seabed, her peaceful expression serenely facing up.

I dress you in sea-colours: turquoise, teal and white. You are occasionally confused for a boy. I don't care. I love you in these colours, your soft skin translucent, cheeks rosy with the delicate blue and green veins in your head a faintly visible pattern under the surface. These tiny capillaries, veins and arteries so discernible through the thin membrane of your skin are a reminder of your fragility. I think of your circulatory system forming while you are inside me, in the tiny ocean of my womb.

How do I help you find your identity? Do you have it now at two weeks, six weeks, nine weeks? Or am I reading too much meaning into the rare smiles and glimpses of temperament that occasionally flash through you? I start referring to myself in the third person, *Mummy thinks this*, or *let go of Mummy's hair*. Who is this new me, Mummy me, that I feel the need to define in this way? Why can't I say 'I' to you? Is it because I'm worried that you don't know who 'I' is? Or that as you begin to understand your own sense of 'I' that my 'I' will become confusing to you? How do we learn to be an *I*? According to Ettinger, the concept of the matrixial is about a perception and understanding of human subjectivity in which we have never been an *I* (child) without a *non-I* (mother); there is no self without non-I. You are not you without me. And now I am not me without you. Your tiny personhood and burgeoning selfhood is changing who I am, throwing aspects of myself into sharp relief while also revealing new parts of my personality. In a new set of circumstances, I learn how *my* self will respond to a range of firsts, new fears, some of the darkest nights moving into the bright normalcy of the day. Like in the ocean, becoming mother is revealing layers of sediment which have lain on my seabed for my lifetime, only now becoming exposed.

CHAPTER 4

Early Days

I GREW UP in an old red sandstone house on a south-facing terrace. It had been built around 1910 and still had a lot of the original features. Some of the tiled fireplaces had been covered with plyboard and wallpapered over before my parents had moved in and rediscovered them. It had mustard walls and brown carpets throughout and one room adorned with Superman wallpaper. The house my parents owned when I was born was in Scotstoun. My parents had lived there for a few years prior to my birth. In fact, my mother had viewed it, arranged and purchased it while my dad was in the USA working on his PhD on the American Labour Movement. Having lived alone for nine months in the theological college accommodation, underweight and distracted, my father returned to Glasgow to live in a house he had never seen before. When I was three months old, they bought the house that was to be our family home for my whole life. My parents tried to sell it three times over ten years and were unlucky each time. The first time was on the cusp of the financial crash and they missed out on selling for a high price. The subsequent times, viewers responded that the house was too big, that it needed modernised and the décor updating, each of these flippant comments wounding my parents who had spent much of their adult lives maintaining and improving the place.

My husband and I had been looking for a flat to move into together for months. We had found one we loved in the Southside of Glasgow, near Queen's Park. It was a lovely park and an area with lots of new eateries and bars. A few years before this, a woman I had met through managing MacSorley's had been horrifically sexually assaulted and murdered in Queen's Park. She used to come to the pub selling cigarettes, then, as the market for this decreased, Britvic bottles of mixer to stock the small fridges below the bar. I managed this pub for a few years while also doing my Masters and various other part-time jobs teaching and tutoring. Moira was warm, pleasant, had a glorious laugh and sense of humour, and always made our short interactions enjoyable with her friendly patter.

The evening she was murdered, Moira and her partner had been out for a drink at *The Gazelle* in Finnieston (now called *The Dirty Duchess*). They should have been staying together that evening, but they had an argument and she went back alone to her flat near Queen's Park.

Fifteen months before he killed Moira, her murderer had amassed 13 convictions. Originally from Slovenia, he had been living in Liverpool and had arrived in Glasgow only ten days before killing Moira. She was parking her Toyota 4x4 near her home when she was accosted. A couple saw them and had a feeling something wasn't right and another couple heard her horrific screams from the park. The husband said to the wife,

'If we hear someone has been murdered tomorrow I won't be surprised.' Neither couple phoned the police and Moira's battered body was found near the derelict bandstand by dog walkers the following morning. She was 40 years old.

Certain details haunted me. One was the argument with her partner. She shouldn't have been there, she should have been at his flat as planned. Wrong place, wrong time. How must he have felt, knowing that their last words had been in anger? That if they had resolved it, she would have awoken tucked up in his bed, safe and sound on the other side of town? I also kept running over the fact that she was seen and heard by two sets of witnesses. Why did they do nothing? I learned about the bystander effect in Higher Psychology, in which we were told about a murder that had taken place in front of a tower block with over 35 witnesses, none of whom called the police (the expectation being that someone else would do it). I had read it in a textbook, but this was it live, real, lived, and with the most awful consequences. People don't want to get involved. What a senseless, awful, devastatingly sad thing to happen.

Ten years on from this, we were looking at a flat in Strathbungo, near Queen's Park. An up-and-coming area, house prices were becoming comparable to the West End. We visited a flat, second floor, cat flap in the close, beautifully furnished with a massive bay window looking out to the park. We both fell in love with it immediately. I appealed to the estate agent, telling them about my four hours' daily commute (between Innellan and my place of work in Glasgow), trying to get them on side. We put an offer in way over the asking price, more than it was worth really, and were told there were seven other offers. In the end, we didn't come close. Even our very best offer was blown out the water. We went back to the drawing board, exhausted at the thought of starting from scratch in the knowledge that it could all come to nothing again. When I told my mum what we were able to borrow in the lead up to the Southside flat bid, she suggested that perhaps we could buy our old family house from her and my dad. I dismissed it immediately: our eyes were on the prize of the Southside place. When it was gone, I returned to this idea, floated it to my husband. Would he like this? Would the house be too loaded with my family history? Or could we make it ours? Could we bring up our children in the house where I grew up? For me, there was something very lovely about this thought, this new way of being in this place again, but this time in the role of parent, not child. The house was being rented out meaning we could not go see it, but we were able to make arrangements to move in as spring arrived. And so, with a sense of history repeating itself, we bought this red sandstone house without my husband ever having set foot in it, the way my mum had bought their last house without my dad seeing it 36 years before.

We moved in in April 2016 and had a blissful week of camping out, no furniture until mine arrived from Innellan, a double mattress on the floor of the guest room (my sister's old room) which was the only room with a pair of curtains still up. I loved it immediately and was surprised by how much remained in my body memory. The particular pattern of creaks on the stairs, I knew these sounds! They were like music to my ears. The bit on the bannister where I got a bad skelf aged around seven. The nooks of the house and garden that had fascinated me as a child, did so no less now. I loved it. I would find myself going to find out the time at the ghost of a wooden clock that my parents had hanging in the living room (1987, it would have been). I sought my reflection in a silver hall mirror that left with my parents in the early 2000s. Even now, I can almost trace the shadow it has left on the Anaglypta and imagine that if it was still there, I would not see a woman in her mid-30s staring back, but instead the same person 20 years younger, a ghost of my earlier presence. I was very much enjoying being back in this place, at once so familiar, surprisingly so, but also with the distance of not having lived in it for over ten years. This is Freud's definition of *Das Unheimliche*, a way of describing the uncanny, literally translated as the home that is also not home. Freud suggests that this also signifies the original home, the womb.

Once we were settled, my husband and I slept in my parents' old room; without realising it, I slept on my mother's side of the bed. I remember, as a small child, rushing through in the mornings to snuggle in beside her. If she was slow to wake, I would use my forefinger and thumb to prise open her eyelids. Her eyeball would be revealed, brown iris, black pupil, not yet focused, still asleep but her eye exposed by my tiny, impatient fingers.

When my sister was born my parents created a system to try to keep me out of their room. A chart drawn on coloured sugar paper was stuck on their bedroom door and for every night I did not go in to their room, I would get a gold star. When I had reached a designated number of stars I was able to select an item of my choosing to celebrate reaching the milestone of whatever arbitrary number of nights they had decided to aim for. I immediately knew I wanted to save for a ceramic swan ornament with diamanté detail on its wing to be added to my collection of 'precious things'. I had clocked it in a shop in Partick and thought it was the most beautiful thing I'd ever seen.

I got the swan and still have it to this day. Along with me, it has returned to the mothership. I had been saving up for my next choice, a coveted typewriter. The detail of exactly how many stars I was going to have to acquire to get this is sketchy but it definitely seemed like a step up from the swan. As beautiful as the swan was, a typewriter was in a different league. At some point during the time when the stars on my chart were mounting up, I decided to give up, since nothing was worth as much as being able to jump into bed next to my parents in the middle of the night and give my mum a cuddle.

This bedroom, a different bed but in the same spot. I lie where she lay, my daughter next to me, as I had lain next to her. I am my mother's daughter, history repeats itself, I am her at a different time, she is me, was me, and my daughter to come, like Russian dolls. Or like migratory birds, following the same patterns instinctually, behaviour ingrained, inexplicably and unquestioningly performing the same actions as the generation before.

I was four when my sister arrived. I was born in March, she was due in April. Because of the age gap there was never any competition between us, I was always the older sister so sibling rivalry never seemed to develop between us. Perhaps because my sister was so ill at an early age I also learned that her life was precious and that she was to be looked after. In all our photos I am pulling her towards me, holding her close. Our closeness has lasted our whole lives and I shamelessly hope that my daughter has a sister to know the joy of this specific bond.

The wallpaper in my parents' room was white, snaked all over with delicate blue vines and tiny blue leaves. The effect was that it was pale blue, icy blue all over. But if you looked closely, you could see the intricate pattern. As a child, I used to imagine the shoots starting at the bottom as though they were growing upwards from the skirting board, each little leaf a step on the ladder reaching upwards to the ceiling. I would trace my finger up the vines as far as I could reach and try to edge the mattress out so I could find the roots, the old wallpaper peeling at the edges at the bottom. I found one of these edges of the paper near the radiator. It was slightly unhinged from its bracket and leaned curiously out from the wall. Next to the radiator knob, the wallpaper was peeling up, the paste having dried out, allowing it to come unstuck. I knelt down on the scratchy, rope-like carpet. I always hated that carpet, sitting on it was punishing and if you knelt on it with knee-high socks on, deep rope-like welts became imprinted in scarlet onto your bare knees. God forbid you ever skidded on it.

Kneeling gingerly, I touched the edge of the paper and tugged gently. The paper began to lift in a satisfyingly uniform straight diagonal line. I paused. Twisting the paper upwards, I could see a dark forest green paper underneath. This had a much larger pattern on it, and only a fragment of a larger damask pattern was visible, the deep green velvety and rich under the lighter floral paper. On touch, it felt mossy, as damp and green as it looked. The tiniest triangle of this corner was poking up from the edge and I pinched this with the nails of my thumb and forefinger. The fragment I had hold of came away suddenly and I held my breath as the soft ripping noise was over in a second. Taking a firmer grip of the dank greenness, I gently tweaked the paper up and away. Moving closer now, I could see a shiny mauve colour. Another layer! This was like pass the parcel, I thought, but with every layer I was imagining the different identities of the room. Who had lived here when it was a deep forest glade, green and shady, rich and damp? Who had lived here when it was a gaudy parlour, like being inside a bubble of blancmange pink? Who had covered over what had gone before with this delicate vine pattern? And why did they leave the previous layers underneath, entombed forever under layer after layer of decoration? Maybe this room had been all the colours of the rainbow. Maybe there were more layers and more under these ones and for every layer that was peeled off, the room would expand, becoming bigger and bigger as it shed its skins like a snake.

I spat on my hand and dampened the green corner, pressing it into the wall. Smoothing it down back into place (minus a tiny bite mark my eager fingers had left) I tried to paste it back to where it had been. The upper layer was more noticeable and I had to curl the edge of the paper the opposite way to encourage it to return to its previously undisturbed state. I leaned back to survey my handiwork. The paper looked a bit grubbier around the edges where I had been touching it, and there was a more noticeable line where the wallpaper had peeled up to, but it looked okay, I thought. I looked around the room again. It was totally transformed now that I knew that the walls held a palimpsest of other identities and lives within it. When I return to the house 30 years later the room is white, the wallpaper painted over. I remember what I found kneeling on the rough carpet as a child. As an adult, I can see the tiny tendrils of the blue vines peeking out from a rip in the wallpaper behind the radiator. I know what is underneath. Nothing goes away really, it is still there, just covered over.

A childhood is so unique, but in the living of it, you have no idea. You have no idea that not everyone has parents like yours. You can't perceive the idiosyncrasies within your own family. You don't understand the eccentricities of the space you grow up in, of your home, and the unique place it will always hold in your memory. Normal is what you know. It is what your family is, and you only realise this when you encounter other families, other homes.

When our daughter was born, the first night in the hospital had been so hard it ended up being the only one. We whizzed through the checks and information so that we could get home with our new baby. Having birthed her at 3.21pm on the Friday we returned home at 4.00pm on the Saturday. I was a mess, still bleeding heavily and moving tentatively with my new surgical scar, but I was delighted to get her home. My sister-in-law came to the hospital and had to help us get her in the car seat as we were so novice. My mum and dad met us at the front door. We took some pictures on the front step, her homecoming.

When she was in my womb, we used to talk to her. 'Who are you?' we would ask my bump. When we were lying in bed excitedly talking about her arrival we would look at each other and ask 'Who *is* she?' In the first weeks of your life we looked for clues as to who you were, your personhood. At three weeks old my husband did a comedy yawn and a first smile flickered across your face. For weeks afterwards, wherever I was in the house, I could hear the roar of comedy yawns coming from the living room, the bathroom, the bedroom as he tried his hardest to replicate the moment of smiling appreciation the first one had provoked.

Two weeks after her birth I received a letter through the mail informing me that I was due a cervical smear test. 'Really?' I thought. 'Give me a break!' At my six-week check-up the doctor said it should be 12 weeks after either a surgical or vaginal birth so there was some respite at least. Nobody told me that even if you don't have a vaginal birth, you still bleed for weeks and months afterwards. Known as lochia, the blood, mucous and uterine tissue leaves your body gradually over a number of weeks. When I asked the midwife at the hospital how long it would last as I stood, hours after the birth, shocked as she lifted one of my legs at a time out of the large, crepe disposable pants I was wearing before thrusting two thick sanitary pads into them, she said, 'it's like a heavy period.' From this I took that it would last five days to a week but it went on and on. A few weeks in I thought it was gone but the next time I went to the bathroom it was back with a vengeance, the sight of the deep red blood provoking a wave of nausea and a tingling in my scar. It was around six weeks after her birth that it stopped for good.

When she was five weeks old, I took her to visit my parents in Dunoon, an old Victorian seaside resort on the Cowal peninsula on the West Coast. They moved there when my dad took early retirement. After a life crafted around work, he was struggling to with what life post-employment was going to look like and seemed on the brink of a crisis of identity. My mother was worried about him 'rattling about' our Glasgow townhouse while she continued to work as a primary teacher. During a chance conversation with a neighbour my dad confessed his uncertainty when asked the question, 'But what will you *do*?' Our neighbour (who had retired years previously) said, 'Think back to what you enjoyed doing when you were a wee boy, then do that.' My dad's childhood summers had been spent (as ours had) on the shingly, rockpool-rich beaches of Kirn, Dunoon and Innellan. His involved messing about on boats and helping out with prepping small vessels to sail. He would get quite maudlin about the dearth of boats on the water and remembered fondly the 'penny boats' which used to litter the West Bay, so-called as it cost a penny to hire one to take out onto the water for an afternoon of adventure. When he thought back to what he loved doing when he was wee, it was to the coast that he wanted to return; not just any coast, but the rocky, shingly, empty beaches of Dunoon where he had spent his childhood swimming, boating and rockpooling.

My parents moved in 2009 and I moved to the neighbouring coastal village of Innellan the year after. My partner at the time and I had wanted to move out of the city, to be in the countryside and to have a garden. We began looking at places 20–30 minutes outside of Glasgow but had not found anything suitable when my partner showed me a picture of a quaint little cottage, by far the prettiest house we had seen. 'Where is it?' I asked. When he told me it was in Innellan, nearly two hours from Glasgow (and a drive, a ferry, a train and a walk away from our places of work in the city centre), I discounted it immediately. However, that weekend we were visiting my parents in Dunoon and thought we would go to view the house, just out of interest. The viewing sealed the deal. The house's charms were even more appealing when stood in the large farmhouse style kitchen of the converted coach house. My dad said, 'It would make a lovely holiday house,' and both he and my mum tried to dissuade us from the move. Although they would be glad to have me nearer (their house was only ten minutes' drive along the coastal road) they felt that the commute would be too arduous, particularly in the winter months. I lived there for six years, and when I moved there, I claimed that I would never not live by the sea again, so much did I love the constant presence of the water. I adored the ever-changing shoreline and the reflections of the sky in the sea. I would get the boat at 6.45am to reach work for 9.00am then make the same two-hour trek back in the evening. At certain times of the year, this was done almost completely in the dark. I often rued that I was not able to enjoy the beauty of the place I lived as I spent so much time travelling there and back. The same faces every morning on the boat, bleary-eyed and clutching coffee canisters and flasks to get them through the journey.

For the first five years of being on the West Coast, the journey was just part of my life, the compromise that made it possible for me to work in a job I loved and live somewhere beautiful. I went through a difficult break-up with my partner and bought him out of his share of the house (with financial support from my parents). Living by myself for the first time, and in a rural location, could be challenging but for the most part I enjoyed it, making fires to burn the bramble branches I had cut in the winter, feeling alone, but strong and free as time helped heal the aftermath of our separation. For the final year that I lived there, the journey became too much. I was stranded for a week in Glasgow, unable to return home as the boats were off due to high winds. I left for work as usual at 6.45am on the Monday morning and could not return that night or the next. By Wednesday I was frantic and desperate to get home. My parents had been feeding my cats but I had to go to H&M before work to purchase new underwear and a clean top and I was frustrated at having to rely on the kindness of friends to put me up in my current displaced state. On the Wednesday evening, Callum (my partner, now husband) offered to drive me to the car ferry after another late night at work and so we gunned it down the motorway to make the final boat. The weather was terrible and rain lashed off the windscreen, making it almost impossible to see the road. What became apparent the further we drove was that the road was very wet. Not just wet, but flooded – the week of storms had taken its toll and the low-lying town of Greenock was like Atlantis, the road a lagoon with orange cones and High Vis signage indicating that it was closed and we could go no further. I burst into tears when I realised that the only other way home was impassable and that I would not get back that evening. In fact, I would not get home until Friday night after 9.00pm, having left for work on the Monday morning before 7.00am. As we drove back up the road to Glasgow, I sobbed quietly while my partner tenderly suggested that perhaps my living situation was becoming a problem. He said that although I put a positive spin on the journey – 'I love it – I can read lots of books!' – I was perhaps a little deluded and the reality of living so far away from work was having a negative impact on my life. Perhaps this would be different now; working remotely has become more possible due to the way in which the pandemic has changed working practices, but at the time, working from home was not an option.

I moved away from the sea in 2016, breaking my vow never to not live near it again. My new life in Glasgow was instantly simpler, with a commute of under 30 minutes rather than two hours each way. I frequently nearly missed my stop on the ten-minute train ride because the journey flew by so quickly,

I couldn't believe I was already there. I missed the presence of the sea in my daily life, its horizontal anchor to the landscape, its salty seaweed smell as I stepped on the early morning boat, the sound of the waves constantly lapping like a metronome, keeping time to my existence. I was sad to admit that the convenience of my new life had taken priority of the romanticism of my sea-life. Having said that, when people exclaimed in delight at the thought of me taking a boat to work, I quickly refuted the romanticism and explained the reality of the dark winter ferries. I still visited Dunoon frequently to visit my parents, and on each iteration of the journey became more incredulous that I had made this voyage every day, twice a day, five days a week, for six years of my life. The four-hour roundtrip between Innellan and my place of work in Glasgow now seemed impossible – so much time spent in transit, in between places, coming or going, on the move. In my new home in the city I enjoyed the luxury of evenings, new time magically created to do as I wished in the time when I would have been shuttling between home and work on my commute.

The first time I took her on the ferry to Dunoon at five weeks old, I noticed a sign next to the muster point, indicating that the boat was breastfeeding friendly. It was just as well, as despite having fed almost continuously during the train ride, when we embarked onto the small passenger ferry she was rooting about, hungry again. I fed her on the boat looking out at the familiar sea and mountains. Despite the usual feeling of being exposed in doing something so primal on public transport, I felt a sense of contentment. My daughter and I were on our way to see my mother and father at their home. My sister was there too. The winter sky was light and reflected off the water as the tiny vessel cut white scars through the surface of the sea. Everyone was excited that she had arrived and I felt so lucky to have this strong net of family woven around me during this vulnerable and raw time. On that initial visit, her first experience of sea air seemed to have had a sedative effect. She slept continuously, huddled like a baby koala onto my dad's expansive, fleece-covered chest.

My father held his clenched fist in front of her face. She looked at his face expectantly and then back to his fist. Slowly he extended one large thumb. One. Her face lit up, she smiled and clapped her hands. He slowly unfurled his index finger. Two. Like the fronds of a fern unfurling, his middle finger peeled back from his fist. Three. She giggled and her own hand twitched. Another digit appeared. Four. Finally his pinky was released from his fist. Five. She was animated now, bouncing up and down where she sat. 'Again?' he asked. She shrieked excitedly. The fist again. One. As his thumb appeared, her own thumb trembled and she pointed it at him. 'Good girl!' he said. Two. This time both their index fingers appeared in synchronicity and she squealed with excitement. Three. Another tiny finger agitated. At four, she was too excited, her chubby hand waving back and forth like a fleshy flag in the wind. At five, he laughed too and picked her up, pressing her soft pink cheeks to his rough, recently shaven face.

My pregnancy had been punctuated with frequent visits to the dentist and then the dental hospital with pregnancy-related gingivitis. The first of these trips to the hospital was before I was 12 weeks and I remember telling the young dentist in hushed tones of my condition, with the caveat that no one is supposed to know yet (these early 12 weeks, the time when you most want and need to tell people to excuse your morning-sickness impeded behaviour but are forbidden to do so). He assured me that my secret was safe with him and that they would not discuss it with anyone else.

My final visit to my own dentist before my daughter's birth was jovial: she was pregnant too! This was her second child and we chatted about how her young daughter was seemingly threatened by the prospect of a new arrival. She was due a month after me but looked so petite and neat that I had not realised she was pregnant until she started the conversation, provoked by my unavoidable swell. As we cheerily waved goodbye, she said nonchalantly that I should make an appointment for the baby when her first tooth came in at about six months. I stopped dead in my tracks as my sense of time lurched forward to begin to comprehend a yawning expanse of time post-birth of appointments and other baby health bureaucracies that I had failed to consider before now. I had been getting through the pregnancy one small section at a time. Even thinking in trimesters was overwhelming. I preferred day-by-day, guided by the bright colours and bite-sized blog posts on my pregnancy app. Thinking about weeks was bearable, again accompanied by a morsel of information and a picture of the corresponding fruit size of my baby (the final fruit was a large watermelon – I shuddered at the thought).

I had only very recently started thinking about the birth, was yet to give any thought to the first weeks of newborn-ness and all of a sudden I saw my future as a lifetime of checking teeth, brushing teeth, making appointments about teeth and for every other body part that my child had.

Ten weeks after her birth I had to go for a dental check-up. My usual dentist was on maternity leave and I enquired after her at the desk. She was well and had given birth to a girl too. Her replacement was a friendly, tall, red-haired man. There was a problem with their generator, he explained, the equipment wasn't working; he could do my check-up but I would have to return the following week for the scale and polish. I flickered with annoyance at the logistics involved in finding another morning to creep out unawares, but shrugged it off. I asked how he was settling in covering for Mairi and he looked at my notes and we got on to the subject of babies. His wife, he informed me, was coming to the end of her maternity leave and they had their own daughter too. I said that, yes, I was enjoying my maternity leave and he indicated that I might not see him again as Mairi was only taking four months off this time.

When I returned the next week, I enquired after how that fateful Monday had been when the generator had broken and was informed cheerily that he had simply taken a half day. He lowered the seat and asked me if I was okay lying down. I responded in the affirmative, yes, I was very comfortable, thank you. We made small talk, my responses occasionally inhibited by his latex-covered fingers inside my mouth. After the scraping, polishing and spitting was done and he was ascending the chair from its recline he asked, 'So, when is your baby due?' This remark proved more painful than the scraping of my gums and I could still taste the metallic taste of blood in my mouth as I answered quickly and quietly 'I have had my baby.' His face flushed up to his red hair as he stumbled over an apology. I fled the dentist's surgery without looking back.

I loudly and comically told my husband about it on my return but my voice was a little too forced, trying to make it funnier than it was. I was actually deeply hurt that I still looked nine months pregnant. It dawned on me that that was why he had asked if I was okay lying back, this was what I was asked throughout pregnancy, at the dentist, at beauticians, at the hospital as after the fourth month the vena cava, a large vein which runs from the heart to the lower body, can endanger the baby if you lie completely flat in pregnancy. I had missed lying flat, lying starfish spread at my parents' house in front of the fire, lying flat out in savasana in yoga for a final relaxing stretch. Apart from this slight on my physical appearance (to be fair, although I had lost two stones of 'baby-weight' – largely the baby herself and accompanying fluids – I still had a way to go), I was perhaps more hurt that the dentist had not remembered the (what I thought was lovely) chat we'd had the week before. I consoled myself that he must have a lot of new patients having taken over all of Mairi's, but the unintended slight and his lack of recollection from the week before still smarted. I looked at myself in the full-length mirror in our room. My legs were trunk-like, no sense of shape above the knee, their girth accentuated by the maternity leggings I was still wearing. I couldn't remember a time when I had not been wearing leggings, but looking at them now I wondered how anything could be less flattering on a post-pregnancy body.

We got into a rhythm of the days, a pattern of sleeping and waking with both her and I being able to get a few hours' of unbroken sleep between feeds in the night. Her first illness, at ten weeks old, was a shock. A few sneezes over the weekend turned into a chesty cough by Monday. She woke at 7.00am for a feed and the hacking cough caused her tiny body to convulse. I had hoped to go to yoga that morning as she had been sleeping later, till 9.00am, so I had been toying with the idea of escaping to an early morning class while she slept. I changed and fed her at 7.00am, my yoga kit in an optimistic pile by the door. I resigned myself to not going. I can't go, she is sick, how could I go? At 7.20am she fell into a deep sleep and I furtively got ready before heading out the door. The December streets were still dark but the sun was rising and I could see the ornate streetlights on University Avenue silhouetted against the yellow-blue light creeping up into the night sky. I had never noticed before how beautiful they were, organic forms cast in iron.

Becoming mother is about becoming remorseful, feeling guilty for the snatches of time you gift to yourself. In this first yoga class after her birth I remembered what my body could feel like, how in warrior two the strength of the body can be felt from grounded feet through to outstretched fingers. My wrists had been painful and weak with tendonitis from picking up my child so I was not sure how strong a foundation my arms would provide for headstand. As my legs floated upwards I could feel my core hardening. 'Well done for finding your new centre of gravity,' my teacher Rosina said. My centre of gravity had shifted throughout the months of pregnancy, her weight growing and her body sinking its weight into my pelvis. I didn't dare do a headstand from the fourth month of pregnancy onwards for fear of toppling over so this first inversion after six months felt different. I thought as I balanced, *my body is different now, it will never be the same*, her passage from me into the world leaving not only physical traces but imperceptible shifts in balance and alignment. Three months before I fell pregnant, I qualified as a yoga teacher. I have been a teacher for many years but teaching this particularly physical practice was a new challenge. I have only ever taught yoga while pregnant, secretly pregnant too, breathless as I spoke the instructions, mindful of my new cargo to keep safe as I lowered my body to the ground.

The yoga felt wonderful but in the final savasana my mind kept wandering home: were they okay? Had she been unsettled and cried the whole time I was away? Why had I come when she was ill and needed me? Was she taking the milk I had blearily expressed before dawn in case she woke up hungry? I rushed home, hurtling through an amber light at the last junction before our street. Flinging my bag into the hallway, I ran up the stairs and into our room. Still dark, curtains closed; she slept serenely in her cot. My husband's face was peeking sleepily out of the white cocoon of the duvet. They had not even noticed my absence, the time I had carved out while the sun was still rising and the day beginning.

The second night of her illness was a return to those early anxious days, of checking the rise and fall of her chest as she struggled each congested breath in and out. The audible snuffles and grunts were reassuring, it was the deeper sleeps, the silences that had me jumping up out of bed to lay my hand on her stomach, to feel her soft warmth as it rose and fell. Even through her illness she was smiling at her daddy in the soft night light, her small face breaking into a sleepy smile as a tiny fist reached for his bare back in the shadows as though to beat it.

Not even her birth, sudden and with a sense of urgency, had prepared me for the strong fear that accompanies a young baby's illness. The need to protect her, to look after her was physically palpable, my body tensed as I cared for her, fed her and soothed her. The mental effects were notable too as I went over and over in my mind the previous week and what failure in my care had allowed her to get ill. I hadn't put a muslin square down on the pillow provided at baby yoga on Wednesday. At baby cinema on Thursday, had I been thorough enough in wiping her hands after being out in public? We let her lie in the living room on a mat with just her nappy on Sunday – had she been warm enough, had she caught a chill? The self-flagellation, self-doubt and self-berating of parenthood were new to me, but I was beginning to recognise how the constant decision making of motherhood requires a new level of responsibility, each action having a consequence that affects the tiny human in your care. Becoming mother is becoming anxious. This anxiety became heightened when she was ill but was always there as a kind of white noise throughout each day. Am I stimulating her enough? Have I sung her enough songs today? Read enough books? I didn't spend time interacting with her when so-and-so was over for lunch/coffee/dinner, will that have impeded her development? Am I taking her out enough? Am I taking her out too much? Is she sleeping enough? And at the right times? Am I taking her to enough baby activities? Is she socialising enough with other babies? Am I giving her enough cuddles and love? Am I speaking to her enough, communicating with her facially, vocally, through touch? Even on days when we have sung all the rhymes and read ten books together I would always think that there are more to be sung, more to be read. The query at the heart of all of these questions is 'Am I any good at this? Am I a good mother?'

When she was three months old, her cheeks took on a rosy hue and she began to blow bubbles while frequently sucking on her fist, my hand, and any other object which hovered near her mouth. The beginning of her teething (as I later found out this was) brought with it a new wave of germ anxiety. Every time she locked her gums around the thumb or forefinger of my father, mother or sister I would grimace. 'I hope your hands are clean!' I would singsong cheerily, while imagining my daughter's tiny mouth opening to meet germs from toilet door handles, rails on public transport, and used hankies. I anthropomorphised the germs. Like the germs in the advert for toilet bleach, I saw them as a horrid, dirty army, invading the pure and previously unplundered land of my daughter's mouth. Even libraries I began to look at as depositories for germs.

Attending a free parent-led Bookbug session, I watched babies older than my daughter launch hard corners of books into wet mouths. Slug trails of drool traced over brightly coloured covers and slobbery fingers grasped for everything. A year later, and this anxiety would take on a different form as the very real risk of catching COVID-19 brought in a new era of concern about sanitisation and the avoidance of sharing space or objects such as toys and books. The germs I worried about initially seem to pale in comparison to the deadly virus that has permeated now over half of my daughter's life.

The strain of her first illness was palpable and both myself and my husband voiced either silently or out loud 'you are not doing that right'. Our critique of each other hung in the air and poisoned it. Resentments built as each of our perspectives became incomprehensible to the other. I begrudged my husband's freedom, his ability to leave the house in the morning with its dishevelled morning messiness, me bleary-eyed and milk-full trying to get everything done before his departure, tethered to the baby, like an anchor, rooting me to one spot for the endless hours of feeding. At work he returned to a semblance of his pre-child existence – while my previous life, my work, hobbies, routines and thoughts were gone forever. That life belonged to someone else that was no longer me. I longed to have had the chance to savour my solo-existence more as I was obliviously living through it. That freedom, the whims on which I would make decisions! Not the endless organising, planning, extraction and guilt that any non-baby related activities now took. In this week of her first illness I was particularly tethered, more acutely housebound for fear of taking my ill baby outside to brave the December chill. Events I had planned to attend hurtled by without me, I stood at the window in the dark winter early evening gazing out into the black, the streets wet and illuminated by the streetlamps, jiggling her incessantly while she howled.

I became jealous of my husband's liberty, his freedom to have a Christmas drink with colleagues after work, his fresh smell of the outdoors when he got home, the enticing odour of his brisk walk clinging to his cold skin. For his part, he was envious of my new slovenly, timeless life, no work to get to, no routine or tasks apart from keeping myself and the baby alive. 'But you get to spend all day hanging out at home with her! I would love that,' he would say. This felt like a blow as it made me feel ungrateful for the time we were having while negating the long, hard, often excruciating repetitions of the moment by moment, hour by hour tedium of childcare. Socks on, socks off. Feed, nappy, repeat. He felt I was lucky to be home all day spending time with our daughter, while he had it hardest as he worked long hours then returned to her screaming red hole of a mouth and demands to be walked around for hours. As I saw it, however exhausting working and being a dad might be, he had the daily rewards of a career and feeling meaningful in the world to colleagues, associates, friends as well as to us. My world had become smaller, less resonant, more insular and insulated. My focus was now one small human. All of my energy was being poured into this new person, while I became more dilute, less formed, paler somehow.

My husband took conversations with other adults for granted. I remembered how he had laughed at my sheer delight when I told him about a car pulling over and asking me for directions when I was on my way to my six-week check-up. My walk through the tree-lined streets was interrupted by a request for help: the two people in the car were seeking the local hospital. I had enjoyed this brief interaction so much. To them, I was just a normal human walking along a normal street, who might be able to help them. They weren't to know that I was a new mother, that this was the first time I had been unleashed from the baby I was tethered to. They needed my help and I gave it to them. I was useful to somebody other than her. I was an active agent in the world again! My delight at this small interaction seemed ridiculous to my husband because it was. He had no concept of *not* being a person in the world, the cushioning from society that his paternity leave had been was a temporary dream state which returning to work had quickly caused to evaporate. My dream state had continued and would continue indefinitely as my old life receded further into the distance. This was my new life, my new reality.

When he came home from work one day I asked how it had gone. Busy as usual, he had launched a new podcast; the film crew who were making a documentary about his company were in, following him about, then interviewing him. He asked about my day. She did three consecutive poos and then had a nap, so I had started clearing out a cupboard. Although I was loving my time with our daughter, it was hard in these conversations not to feel inferior due to having become mother.

My world was the house, my main companion a currently near-silent baby (apart from the bouts of screaming), and because of this my conversation, my chat about the day-to-day of my life which had always felt so equal with my husband, seemed diminished. I felt it again a few weeks later when we were out for dinner, him holding her on his lap as we ate pizza. All I had to offer the conversation were reflections on her. Had he noticed that thing she had started doing with her eyebrows? Wasn't she much better now she was nearly over her cold? What sort of night would she have, as she had napped a lot that day? I clung to my island of her while he remained on the mainland, his talk of work and meetings as alien to my experience as mine of childcare and home was to him. Having a child diverts a couple from the path they are on, simply because the day-to-day experience of the main caregiver becomes antithetical to that of whoever continues to work.

That our positions grew further apart should not have been surprising, but it was. The rift of how different our daily ways of being had become felt like a disruption. My days started before light: preparation, expressing milk, silent chores before the baby wakes, a long day of mothering then exhaustion and the need for sleep causing oblivion from 8.00pm. The guilt of a last mouthful of a cup of tea snatched before hurtling towards her cot to pick her up. The tiny five-minute jobs that would take me weeks to do. I intend to cut her nails for a week and a half but it was only when she scratched her face that I finally looked out the tiny nail clippers and gingerly cut her nails. I cried when I cut her pinkie nail too low exposing the vulnerable red raw flesh underneath. I found time to eat only when she was feeding. A toast crumb in her eye. A grain of rice on her fist, chocolate on the seat of her new white tights, curry on her sleep suit, coleslaw down her back. His day would start later: stories with our daughter before leaving for work, a long day of meetings, managing people, meeting deadlines, then returning for some fatherly interactions at night-time. Our circadian rhythms became out of sync, we were off kilter and we couldn't quite get back in step no matter how hard we tried.

Both of us experienced amnesiac nights. After he returned to work and I was doing the night feeds alone, he would put her down at night while I got some sleep when he got home from work. He would wake up the next morning and ask me, 'How was your night?' I would try to think back to what had happened; I would know that I had fed her and changed her nappy, sometimes multiple times, but my memories were intangible. 'I don't know,' I would say dully, 'I can't remember.' I would ask him, 'How was your night, when did you get her down?' He would look blankly back at me, propped up in bed, and say, 'I don't know, I can't remember.' These amnesiac episodes were a symptom of tiredness and our bodies trying to get used to the new rhythms and patterns of a routine not yet established. We were slaves to our baby in the first weeks home after her birth and we passed the nights in a dreamlike state, catering for the most basic of human needs – food, warmth, love – into the wee small hours.

When my husband was working late and I had sole responsibility for bedtime, I would find myself shushing to the rhythmic pattern of the 'shusher', an orange and white plastic device designed to mimic a human making the shushing sound (which is itself supposed to replicate the internal swooshing and swirling noises of the mother's digestive system audible in the womb). For hours on end I would imitate the sound of a machine imitating a human in an attempt to send her to sleep. That neither the shusher or my shushing were effective reminded me that the baby didn't care how much money or time went into any of these strategies for stopping crying and magicking sleep, these things were on her terms alone.

Someone I know told me that her baby's crying had got so bad, she had closed the door of the nursery and walked away. *I sit with you in the dark as you cry, speaking my thoughts to you in a low, soft voice. Do you know, at ten weeks that I am there all the time? Do you know that I will never leave you? I whisper these things to you in the night, as your hot sweet breath warms my ear. 'I've got you,' I say to you, 'I've got you.' And I mean it.*

If she coughed, I checked her. And I wondered, should her hands be so cold? Was there a slight dampness in the air? When she was a few weeks old I found mushrooms growing out of the new grey carpet in the nursery. A drip from the radiator had created a deliciously moist atmosphere for the growth of fungi. I was horrified. The nursery was out of bounds. She lay in the middle of our king size bed, like a raft in the middle of the ocean. Despite the size of the bed there was no way to lie comfortably next to her or around her without disturbing her, so I would ease myself gingerly onto the edge of the bed and hover perilously trying to sleep but unable to because of my position. Her tiny body dominated the bed, her presence resonating through the room, every part of the house full of her, her smell, her paraphernalia, her toys, clothes, books. Her reach extended to the car, her car seat and nursery CDs, books and blankets littering the back seat. And her tentacles infiltrated both grandparents' houses with playmats and colourful baby bouncers invading their serene, neat homes, lying dormant and inanimate until her next visit.

Having slept on the opposite end of the bed for a week so that I could lie face to face with the baby in her cot to monitor her breathing in the night, her illness seemed to be abating. On the eighth night I woke up with the wind howling outside. Her sweet lips fluttered in sleep, dream smiles flashed across her placid face. She looked angelic but the grunts and snuffles that emanated from her sleeping form were more like that of a little piglet than a child. I couldn't sleep and sent my pillow upwards to the headboard and manoeuvred up to where my husband was lying. I pressed the back of my body into the front of his and he opened his arms from their duvet cocoon to wrap them round me. The curve of my spine nestled into his belly and in this 5.00am embrace I found the edges of myself once again.

As Christmas approached, my husband's grandmother became ill. She had known before anyone that I was pregnant, before even we did. The Christmas day prior while our niece (her great granddaughter) was opening her presents she had asked loudly, 'When are you having one?' My husband thought I had politely ignored her but I genuinely didn't hear what she'd said. When we visited her next and I was, indeed, pregnant, she said conspiratorially that she had known I was pregnant, that she had sensed it. Later she told me I was having a boy called David and that I would have two boys. At the time I was convinced I was having a boy so I took her word for it.

We took our daughter to visit her when she was four weeks old. We had wanted to take her sooner but the drive to Kilmarnock was longer than the recommended time in the car seat for babies under a month. We stopped on the way and I bought yellow and red roses, the colours bleeding into each other on each petal, bright, loud and autumnal. When we arrived his nana was wearing red trousers and a yellow blouse and she looked like the flowers. I put them in a vase next to her armchair and we gave her the baby, three autumns together in the small white room.

She repeated, 'It's been years since I held a wean like this,' as my daughter nuzzled into her. She was registered as blind and how much of the baby she could see was dubious, but she could smell her and feel her and breathe her in. She told us about her new house, another in the sheltered housing estate she was currently in but ground floor, main door and with a little courtyard with benches outside it where the residents could sit in the summer and chat and play cards when the weather was nice. 'Beautiful,' she said, 'just beautiful.' As we were leaving she took us round to see it, the short walk punctuated by frequent rests on her walker as my daughter wailed.

Days before Christmas she was taken to hospital. We visited her in Kilmarnock, in the hospital near where she stayed.

Her face looked sunken, her mouth caved in under the mask of the nebuliser. My husband asked his dad about her teeth, he had never seen her without them. She had had them all out when she was pregnant over 50 years ago. The hospital was the same one where my husband had watched his grandfather, her husband, die 17 years before. 'When you lose your man, that's it,' she had said at the time but then lived on, like all the women in his family, making a new solo life for themselves, these dour yet incredibly sharp West of Scotland women. She passed away two days before Christmas. A life beginning, a life ending. The plans which would not be followed through, the baby she wouldn't see grow, the summer sitting on the bench in front of her house that would never come.

CHAPTER 5

Other Mothers

AT BABY YOGA we would sing 'Wind the Bobbin Up', 'Oh The Grand Old Duke of York', 'See-Saw Margery Daw', 'Round and Round the Garden'. As I remembered all of these rhymes from my own childhood, it stuck me how little had changed in the years since I was a baby. The same bright colours and simple rhythms are key to all baby activities. My own mother was reassured that the things that she did instinctively are now government-sanctioned policy. Hold your baby. Read to your baby. Talk to your baby (not just in a baby voice). Touch your baby. Sing to your baby. Look at your baby. My mum had sung 'Boogie Woogie Baby' to my sister and I when we were small and now my daughter experienced the same exercise regime, her arms and legs being pumped up and down to my mother's energetic singing.

Back in their size eight leggings and neon workout tops, the other mothers would chat before class. 'How was the birth?' 'Really easy. Only took me 90 minutes.' 'No bother at all.' While this relentless positivity is admirable in some ways, it can be ostracising to those of us who were not able to 'birth' in the traditional (vaginal) sense, or for others, like one mother I meet at baby yoga, whose 42-hour labour could not be described in any way as 'really easy'. This may also be typical of West-of-Scotland women – putting a brave face on things that are actually very tough.

Often I am the outsider. At baby yoga, one mum made a joke about how her son had missed his wake window. Everybody laughed. I didn't know what a wake window was. I looked around the room; everyone looked young, they were all wearing Lycra, thighs trim and toned, their pink fluorescent tops and grey exercise gear clinging to flat stomachs. There were no saggy mum tums apart from mine, which still looked like a sack tied loosely in the middle, a mysterious dent having appeared between my upper and lower abdomen. Their breasts were pert and when they lowered their bra to breastfeed their breasts didn't flop out and descend another four inches as though fleeing the brassiere. How were they doing this? I thought. Full faces of make-up, lipstick glossy and freshly applied, babies beautifully dressed and sleeping through the mum yoga bit so they all get to focus on their own bodies for a while. Some would wake their babies up for the baby yoga section where they lay docile and giggling, other mums would put on a lavender eye mask and indulge in some me time. How were they doing this? Apart from me and one or two other women, you would not know this group of slim, manically positive women had just entered motherhood. There were exceptions, of course: the GP I met at baby yoga who confessed to feeling stupid about phoning her health visitor thinking 'she should know what to do', the mum who wanted to drink a glass of wine while breastfeeding without judgement.

My circle of mothers expanded. We debated when to take them swimming, those that had done it able to pontificate on which pool was warmest and how long to stay in for. The local leisure centre runs a drop-in class called 'ducklings' for £4 while a nearby hotel runs 'Water Babies', which is £170 for ten classes and a complimentary photoshoot. One of the mums admitted to me that the free photoshoot is caveated with the statement that to buy the photos it is £199 for three. Granted they are underwater shots (I immediately thought of the Nirvana *Smells Like Teen Spirit* album cover), but the crass commercialisation of these first moments made me feel uneasy. By constructing a full itinerary for my daughter I convinced myself that she was doing enough activities to aid her development. But did I just buy into the baby-money-making machine? Was I just another unsuspecting consumer who played into the hands of capitalist forces?

This transient set of relationships was the first substantial group of new people I had met in years. A friend who was internet dating bemoaned the fact that when you reach your mid-30s, you rarely meet new people. Unless you take up a new hobby or evening class (as I have done in the past), you tend to stick with the old faithfuls – friends from school or university, some cool work colleagues that you have enough in common with to make time to see them outside of work, and family. Who has time to meet new people? And how do you do it without the buffer of everyone being in the same boat (new at secondary school, new at university) or bound together by the shared experience of a workplace? How do you even make friends anyway? I realised that for the clan of new mums I have met, we were all bound together by this newness. We had been cast adrift on the good ship motherhood and were novice sea-women trying to work out how to steer the vessel.

I would have a bath in the morning with Autumn lying on the bathroom floor on her elephant playmat striking the brightly coloured objects dangling down within her reach. A flashing chicken was out of reach, emanating jovial music while the lights danced around its spots (do chickens have spots?). I would have the shower door ajar so I could see her as I lay in the steaming bath, listening to her shrieks of joy as she flayed her limbs at the objects, hoping the shrieks would not descend into a cry. Morning was my bath-time but by teatime I would find myself longing for another bath, another purging in hot water to end the day. Once her harness was removed I had to bathe her at night and after the initial glee of this, it became a chore. I became envious of her cheery soak in the tub before bedtime, wishing it was me who was being bathed, pyjamaed, fed and put to bed.

At four months her feeding was efficient, her lips find-ing my nipple like a homing pigeon and her gulps deep and long. By that time I had mastered the art of subtle breastfeed-ing with a variety of nursing tops and dresses, but her feed-ing had become awkwardly audible as she worked to drain my breast. As she gained strength she began to show signs of some agency. When we tried, unsuccessfully, to bottle-feed her with expressed milk, a depressing nightly ritual which we all grew to dread, she would thrust her fists up to hit the bottle as though trying to push it away, her eyes flashing with indignation and the intention clear: 'I DON'T WANT THAT.' She had become a person, a person with moods and needs and agency.

There was the odd day of fatigue, despair, the desire to crawl out of my skin and into another life. Not frequent but severe enough when they occurred to shock me. When the health visitor came at around eight weeks post-birth, she asked me to fill out a questionnaire about how I had been feeling – an assessment for postnatal depression. I filled it out, thinking of other mothers and how they might be doing.

My husband and I were both besotted by her. No one else was a part of our joy with this human we had created. Her grandparents and our families adored her but only her dad and I were in this tiny familial bubble of love. At four months old she also found her voice. Crying had been happening consistently since she was born but it was almost as if she was unaware that the tiny wail was coming from her. On one of our first outings to a restaurant I was paranoid about her crying disturbing other diners. When my husband took her from me and held her to him the sound was almost inaudible. Her tiny lungs' maximum volume was minimal. At four months, her lungs were bigger, her vocal cords more developed and her awareness of herself improved. She seemed to understand now that some sounds emanated from her and was keen to experiment with noises. These varied from blowing constant raspberries (accompanied by saliva bubbles) to full pitched screams. The raspberries were from my mother as she continually blew them on my daughter's neck when she visited. Part way between a kiss and a provocation, she had learned that these were part of a system of communication and vocalised with them frequently. I told my mum this over the phone and she seemed delighted. This coincided with my daughter teething which made me wonder if there was something soothing or comforting about this. Perhaps the vibrations on her gums felt nice as she did it.

My daughter would cry when the car was stopped at traffic lights, was peaceful when it was in motion. Like the Keanu Reeves movie *Speed* (except with a tiny human instead of a bomb), we had to keep the car constantly moving. Car journeys became a complex attempt to avoid all of the traffic lights in the area, or, upon stumbling on one, whizzing through the amber light full throttle to avoid the car stopping and the inevitable (and surprisingly loud) wails that would begin to emit from her tiny body.

The screams were alarming, sometimes crescendo-ing from a squeal, other times just out of the blue, piercing the silence. I would rush to her but nothing was wrong, she was not in pain or even crying, she was just testing this new bit of machinery she realised she had. She would often babble along with her books or while I was speaking to her, narrating our days as I had begun to do. These conversations we had felt meaningful even in this pre-language stage. She was beginning to understand that her voice was a tool, a way of drawing attention towards her, of making herself understood.

By the time she was four months old we had a routine of baby classes and activities as I attempted to ensure she was getting enough stimulation and contact with other babies. On Mondays, my aunt took her out for a big walk in the morning; on Tuesdays we attended baby sensory, a free-for-all of disco lights, bubbles, textures and noise; on Wednesday mornings we went to baby yoga; and on Thursdays my husband was off so we would occasionally attend Watch with Baby at the Grosvenor Cinema or sometimes stay home and play until he went to work at 5.oopm. On Wednesday afternoons my mother-in-law would take her and on Friday mornings my parents would have her. This routine of sorts seemed to suit us both well, it was a good compromise of activities for her and hours here and there where I could have a break from caring for her to catch up on housework or do some work and some writing.

Baby sensory classes were thematic – the first week was 'weather' so the facilitator had a range of objects to represent thunder and rain, and we all held the edges of a large sheet with silver foil attached and fluttered it to embody lightning. While every week was different, the consistent aspects of the classes were the main hall strip lights being turned off and the 'baby disco' lights being turned on. These were a series of red and green dots which danced frantically around the floor and walls while music played and the babies cooed. At the first class, I reflected that this was as close to a nightclub as I was going to get for the foreseeable future. The babies did seem to enjoy the shift in atmosphere. The other repeated element was bubbles – the facilitator would scoot around the outside of the circle with a bubble machine, filling the space with 'magical bubbles'. My daughter seemed nonplussed by these, but when one burst in her face I found myself anxiously hovering my hands in front of her head when the bubble machine was on to avoid soapy liquid getting in her eyes. Perhaps this diminished her experience of bubble time but they popped and dispersed so quickly it was hard to tell. Apart from the weekly ritual of bubbles and lights that transcended any theme, the rest of the classes were made up of various noise-making implements: one week the rattles for mum and baby were for rain; the next when we were doing 'sound' as a theme, we were furnished with the rattles (a small one for baby and a large one for mummy), a metal lid from a biscuit tin, a plastic basin and one chime from a xylophone. All of the mums and babies crashed and thrashed about while a backing track played pointlessly. The cacophony was not rhythmic or tuneful but as I watched my daughter try-ing to clench her fist around the baby rattle, which was slightly too heavy for her to hold, a determined look on her face, I felt I could see her brain working trying to calibrate the hand-eye coordination needed to evoke a sound from this bright green plastic object.

Every class would begin and end with a signed song – say hello then say goodbye. I had been reading about the benefits of baby sign language in a chapter of *Superbaby* (although as an American text it discusses American Sign Language (ASL) as opposed to British Sign Language (BSL)). I was keen to learn this to provide a way of communicating early and to estab-lish a pre-language way of facilitating conversation with my daughter, but found myself at bath-time muttering 'What is the sign for 'duck'?' as I tried to sign 'Five Little Ducks Went

Swimming One Day'. It is quite a crucial sign for the song, so I found myself improvising with the light-up rubber ducks that my mother-in-law had bought for when we had to go to the hospital for bath-time. In the first weeks of baby sensory classes, my daughter would ignore me entirely as I signed to her, instead twisting her head and body in an arch away from me to gaze at baby Finn next to her. She was much more enamoured with the other examples of her species at these classes than any of my over-enthusiastic attempts to engage her in learning and development activities.

I started eating my evening meal at 4.30pm, the baby massage, bath-time, and bed process beginning at 6.00pm and ending indefinitely depending on how many times I needed to go up to feed and resettle her. I realised too late that I had made a rod for my own back in terms of allowing her to fall asleep at my breast every time. It was the only way it could happen, the only way it could be done. Apart from the crying, but I couldn't take the crying. I read my baby books shamefully knowing that I was flying in the face of advice from (real) doctors. We just wanted her to get to sleep. When everyone was asleep except me, I would hear gentle snores from the other side of the bed and from her cot next to my side of the bed. Surround sound breathing, the inhale and exhale of sleep, his deeper, louder, more resonant, hers lighter, little lungs holding less air, still audible on the in and out breath as she sleeps.

I developed a painful condition in my hands and wrists called De Quervain's Tendonitis. It is a repetitive strain condition common in mothers also known as 'mummy thumb'.

It is exacerbated by the constant manoeuvring needed for caring for a baby and is intensified by breastfeeding as often the weight of the baby's head lies across the wrist. In the mornings my condition was at its worst, the first nappy change of the day a painful battle as my stiff hands struggled to uncatch the sides of the nappy, lift her wriggly legs by the ankle and remove the weighty nappy, heavy from her long night of sleep. She was excitable in the morning, vocalising and thrusting her hands and legs in the air. Occasionally, she would kick her legs hard while lying on the changing table, her heels connected with the swollen and tender tendon of my right hand. The shockwave of pain would jar from my wrist through my whole body and it was all I could do not to scream.

You cried. I held you. You struggled. I cuddled you close. You dragged your tiny sharp nails down my cheeks, fingers splayed, grasping at my skin desperately, you don't realise that you are hurting me, that my skin is delicate and not as malleable as you think it is. It's another surface to you, perhaps a plaything.

During the Easter holidays, when the usual itinerary of classes paused, the days felt even more lawless than usual. I arranged to meet another mother for a walk and we decided to go to a Bookbug session at the library. When I met up with her she had invited her neighbour and her wee girl too. When we arrived, the session was busy, and there were around 40 babies on the floor, on laps and toddling around the brightly carpeted space. I slipped my daughter out of her snowsuit and my friend's neighbour commented 'Oh we have those pyjamas too!' I flushed with embarrassment. I had hoped that the new pyjamas one of my husband's colleagues had bought for her would pass as clothes with their bright colours and giraffe design but hadn't bargained on being in an environment with so many other mothers. I mumbled something about how I was struggling with clothes because of the tendonitis in my wrists and that sleepsuits and pjs were the best option. Becoming mother is becoming ashamed of not meeting the standards of other mothers.

A woman with twins was breastfeeding both of them when we arrived, balancing both babies using a large flat breastfeeding pillow. Her other son was there, playing in the middle with the other older children. He looked about three and had a green chair with him that he was moving around and sitting on. His mother had finished breastfeeding the twins and was changing them on the carpeted floor. She called the boy over and he dutifully brought his little green chair to sit closer as the session progressed. She admonished him twice about swinging on his chair. I looked to my daughter to see how she was progressing with her rice cake, it was almost gone, the sticky globules of pink smeared on her chin. In an instant the boy on the chair toppled over and landed on the head of one of the twin babies on the floor. There was a stunned silence and the baby began to wail. I felt sick. The woman grabbed her baby and with her other hand comforted her three-year-old, who had also begun to sob uncontrollably. I became overwhelmed with a number of feelings. Wanting to help but not knowing how to do it. Feeling traumatised from witnessing an accident.

Realising the precarity of everything. Fearing future accidents, trying to foresee them. Becoming mother is trying to have the power of premonition to avoid bad things happening. But they do. (The baby was fine – I saw the family 18 months later, during the pandemic, in Kelvingrove Park. The twins were wearing brightly coloured snowsuits and chasing their older brother, cheeks rosy in the winter sunshine).

I didn't like to breastfeed after having more than one small beer. I felt people judge me and also that my inhibitions were lowered in a way that maybe they shouldn't be.

We take you to Bruges so I can present at a conference when you are seven months old and we visit the Beer Experience. You are the only baby at the Beer Experience. Daddy wears you in the Ergobaby and you are so tired that even your obsession with the iPad, which is used to guide us around the large warehouse, can't stop you from falling asleep. At the end of the tour we can use our three tokens to try three beers. I try one and then decide not to have more as the strong Belgian beer is too much for me. We decide to donate our tokens to other visitors and leave them with two young women who have just arrived. As we go to leave, my husband's peripheral vision is hindered by your body in the Ergobaby and he trips over the leg of a bar stool. We laugh, abashed, as people turn to look at us. 'It looks liked you tripped because you are drunk,' I say. 'I know,' he says. We leave the Beer Experience and worry if it was okay to have brought a baby to it.

How is she six months old already? The time seems to have passed so quickly but at the same time it's like she has always been here. Her activity levels have intensified and she is on the move constantly. When I met friends I hadn't seen since her birth, they would tell me 'she is a very busy baby'. Legs pumping, fists banging, mouth moving, scanning the room for things to touch, to grab, to gnaw. When laid on the floor she would roll and roll until an object or piece of furniture stopped her, causing her to shriek in frustration and one of us to lift and reset her so she could repeat her rolls.

As my tendonitis worsened, I couldn't write or type on my phone. Scrolling through social media exacerbated my 'mummy thumb' and I began to watch documentaries on iPlayer on my iPad with headphones while lying in bed breastfeeding to pass the time. I watched Louis Theroux's *Louis and the Nazis* and was fascinated by the 11-year-old singing duo Lynx and Lamb who are being brought up as racists by their mother. Watching these young girls give the Nazi salute, and talk about shooting Black people on their white-supremacist created computer game *Ethnic Cleansing* (as their mother encourages them and makes them bologna sandwiches), I was struck by how clearly I saw a part of motherhood for what it is: the instilling of your own values into the lives of your children. While their mother April's views come across as abhorrent, the vision of a woman bringing up her daughters to embody, enact and reiterate her own worldview is evident. Lynx and Lamb (also known by their duo stage name *Prussian Blue*) act as miniature spokespeople for a racist movement that they are perhaps too young to comprehend. When will my daughter be old enough to question me? Will I have enabled her to have the tools to make up her own mind? What views will we share and where will we differ? Will I be able to accept a deviance, defiance or denial of the values I hope to instil in her? Can we remain close even if she chooses another path? What if she becomes someone I disagree with? What if she becomes racist or violent or holds political beliefs I think are repugnant? Or if she is an uncompassionate person, or cold, or selfish? How can I find a way of sharing the values I think are important in life while still giving her agency to find her own way?

I began to notice that all of her books, toys and playthings represented the natural world. From her rainforest Jumperoo to her ocean creature counting blocks, farmyard cuddly toys and her bedtime story 'Say Goodnight to the Sleepy Animals', so much of what she encountered was from the natural world. The more-than-human inhabitants of the earth are her first playmates, first learning tools and reference points. How can we start like this and end up caring so little for anything non-anthropocentric? When do we stop caring for the animals we hold so dear in childhood?

I panicked about plastic. I started noticing the profusion of plastic in my daughter's life. Not just in the disposable nappies, nappy bags, nappy bin liners, bottles, teats, soothers, teething rings, toys, furniture, and bath toys, but more insidiously disguised in the soft things that are skin-close. The synthetic fabrics of her clothes, the soft blanket which is plastic in disguise, a wolf in sheep's clothing, pretending to be soft and cosy and natural, when it is plastic by another name. I shuddered to think of the chemicals already inside her tiny body, the plastic poisoning having begun in utero.

One Saturday night I promised my husband a cocktail evening once our daughter was down. I made espresso martinis, two parts vodka to one Kahlua and a shot of coffee. We were out of ice so the almost pure alcohol was unpleasantly lukewarm and I struggled to get the creamy foam head on the mix from shaking it. We sipped wine as we waited for ice to freeze. The cold version was much improved but still tasted toxically boozy. As I drank the last of the dark brown, sticky liquid we heard a sharp cry from the baby monitor. Her white limbs flailed in distress. She had been sleeping through till 4.00am most nights. It was 9.10pm. My husband went up to settle her but I joined him a moment later as her cries ceased to abate. He changed her nappy as her panicked wail continued. He tried to soothe her but she was inconsolable. Our eyes met over her tiny head in the dim light of our bedroom. We both knew I was going to have to feed her. As I lowered myself into the bed slipping in beside her she grabbed hungrily for my breast. I thought about the mother orca who carried her dead infant for 17 days. The baby was likely to have died of poisoning from the mother's milk, contaminated by a combination of industrial chemicals and hormone-altering plastics. My milk was poison, I was contaminated. Desperate to pull my breast from her mouth, I imagined alcohol entering her bloodstream, her tiny capillaries coping with toxins from my body. In *The Argonauts*, Maggie Nelson speaks of the 'toxic maternal', acknowledging that human breast milk now contains actual poison, from paint thinners and cleaning fluid, rocket fuel and flame retardants. She says that infants do not get to choose, that they take what they can get to ensure survival. The feed was thankfully short, for comfort more than hunger and I crept back downstairs. Becoming mother is becoming torn, between attempting a return to normal life and the reality that attempting the return has a price, one that rarely feels worth paying.

CHAPTER 6

Perambulating

IN THE FEBRUARY sunshine I walk so that my shadow shields your eyes from the sun. I walk with you in my shadow manoeuvring myself around the pram to avoid you squinting into the sun. When you nap it's like pressing a reset button. You fall asleep cranky and exhausted, you wake up smiley and bright.

I am a perambulater, 'a person who walks, especially for pleasure and in a leisurely way'. I perambulate around Glasgow like I never have before, rediscovering the city in these long free days and visiting its many museums.

Doing the same walk each day I noticed the ways in which the flowers and plants were changing with the seasons. First, the snowdrops appeared, their delicate lampshade heads nodding in the still harsh February wind. Then, the crocus, their purple, white and yellow flutes gazing open-mouthed at the sun. In late March the army of daffodils appeared, blazing yellow streaks through the centre divides of dual carriageways and roadsides. We visited Victoria Park, where the yellow flowers appeared unabashedly vivid against the green grass. When I was younger, we visited the park a lot, walking through it to Whiteinch Library. We entered from the underpass then followed the swooping road which elevated us above the park. The flowerbeds were always spectacular, circular sections in the centre abundant with colour but, most impressively, the semi-circular sloping beds like rising suns made up of intricate designs and tributes to the city. 1988 was the year of the garden festival in Glasgow: that year and those following were most impressive in terms of the floral displays. Years later council budget cuts left the beds unplanted, black gaping wounds of exposed soil scarring the grass.

When I took my daughter to Victoria Park in January the pond was frozen and the beds were empty and bleak. A few months later, the spring after she was born, I inhaled sharply when I reached the top of the incline and saw the beds resplendent with hyacinths. The intake of breath was not only due to their vivid colours, each bed a block of purple, yellow, blue or pink, but also because of the sweet smell that was carrying in the wind. Walking through the flowers with the pram I tried to see if there was any change in my daughter's expression as we meandered through the heady aroma. Japanese poets frequently refer to an 'autumn aroma', the smell of the matsutake mushrooms which are renowned for their pungent smell. In *The Mushroom at the End of the World*, Anna Tsing writes: 'It's not an easy smell. It's not like a flower or a mouth-watering food. It's disturbing. Many people never learn to love it. It's hard to describe. Some people liken it to rotten things and some to clear beauty – the autumn aroma. At my first whiff I was just... astonished.' While the spring hyacinths are invariably sweet, the intensity of the fragrance can also have a sickly effect. Too much of a good thing momentarily overwhelms the senses. I am astonished at their pungency. My daughter seemed unfazed.

As the daffodil heads withered, the tulips appeared and I noticed the camellia had lasted longer in bloom this year. Scarlet once described this to me as the 'Alice in Wonderland flower,' its perfect bud opening into an impossibly perfect and extraordinary pink bloom. On close inspection, the capillaries of the flower could be seen delicately running through it, a darker pink thread branching from the centre of the petals outwards. Like the veins on my daughter's head, this intimate understanding of the flower as something living, with processes of vitality happening under the skin strikes me.

The yellow forsythia and early blossoms appear at the same time, the yellow and pink complementing each other. Then, at the end of April, came the cherry blossoms. I look forward to this every year as the city is transformed into an exotic place because of the shades of pink that adorn many of the trees. As though they have been in disguise all year, as normal green-leafed trees, in April, like butterflies emerging from cocoons, their blossoms appear. Primarily they are a soft, light pink, but there are also white apple blossoms and darker pink blossoms, and the combination of all three in my local park takes my breath away the first day I see them. Since before my daughter was born, I had imagined taking pictures of her with the blossoms, such a marker of the time of year are they. When they began to bloom I took her on her walks three times a day and looked up at the soft pink canopy of flowers. I texted my sister-in-law with a couple of photos and said we should take some pictures of our girls with the blossoms. I didn't take any photos of my daughter myself as it would have meant stopping the pram, which she objected to noisily. My parents came to stay the night and I told them the route they must take the next day when they took Autumn on her walk. That night was unseasonably cold, blustery, the wind howling through the gaps in our windows making an eerie noise all night. After they left I took my daughter out. We walked down my favourite street, the avenue of blossoms. The street looked as though it had been turned upside down. Instead of a canopy above my head, there was now a carpet below. Soggy pink petals became glued to the wheels of the pram turning them into floral wreaths. I looked up. Some blossoms still clung to the branches but the trees had been decimated. Strangely, I felt a kind of grief. The blossoms I had looked forward to all year are gone. They lasted less than a week. I didn't get pictures of my daughter with the blooms, the moment had passed, I missed it. Why did I feel so sad about this? Was it the waste of the beauty that was there so fleetingly? The sense of time passing beyond my control? I trundled her pram through the sea of pink petals, each one the shape of a tear as I tried to get her to sleep.

As I walked the familiar streets, I would look in people's gardens. Some opted for slabs or stones and the greenery was minimal, but some, even small gardens, were brimming with colour and life. The garden with the giant tulips, red and yellow striped that reminded me of the ones we had in our front garden when I was a child. The garden with two pink pieris, their flamboyant pink leaves visible all the way down the street. In our front garden there is a Japanese maple. My aunt Linda from America gifted it to my mum and dad when they lived in the house over 20 years ago. What started as a shrub is now an elegant tree, its red leaves refracting the light into our front room during the spring and summer months. It is so tall now that the top of it is visible from our bedroom window a storey up, its delicate, red, spindly leaves shaking in the wind. I love this tree and in autumn, when it loses its leaves within the space of a few days, feel sad to see its naked black branches silhouetted against the sky, signalling that winter was on its way.

I went from travelling huge distances each day to covering the same lengths by tramping the same circuit of streets around our house. This was partly practical – if she fell asleep quickly I was close to home. I could go back and read or write or cook with her sleeping in her pram. It was also because I liked this growing sense of knowing this place. I knew it well already, these were the streets in which I grew up, where I played on long summer nights chasing ice cream vans and riding bikes. They were the streets on which I did my first paper round, age 11 and embarrassed when I could not fit the huge Sunday papers in the tiny letterboxes. I tried to identify which ones they were, which house it was that had the dog that barked at me and frightened me every time. The streets by the allotments where my dad had an allotment for 20 years, where my sister and I spent what felt like punishing weekends digging, weeding and picking raspberries (and which now seem idyllic).

These were the streets I walked to school and then to work, the places I have known all my life. But I know them differently now, they have taken on a new quality by the every-day-ness of my sojourns along these pavements.

When Autumn was seven months old I got ill. I had had a few sniffles in the preceding months but this was the first full-blown-can-hardly-move-never-mind-care-for-a-child kind of ill. It had been working on me all weekend but I had powered through, ignoring it. Saturday had been my daughter's first march for Scottish independence and we spent the morning at Kelvingrove Park as part of a team handing out 10,000 newspapers. After stopping for lunch we took the train to Glasgow Green where a sea of Saltires blew in the spring breeze. The weather had been kind (particularly for our task, no one wants to be handed a soggy newspaper in the rain) and there was a festival feel to the gathering in the green with live music and speakers. My throat throbbed malignantly throughout the day and I hoped the takeaway curry we got for dinner would help clear my sinuses. Sunday was busy with chores, visits and childcare and when I was mopping the living room at 7.00pm a wave of weakness hit me. Oh no, I thought.

Monday morning, I was flat on my back and could hardly move. My head throbbed and my entire body felt weak. After a few phone calls we had arranged for my aunt to take the baby in the morning as usual, with my mother-in-law taking her in the afternoon. As soon as she was gone, I fell into a deep sleep, waking only when my alarm went off before they arrived home at lunchtime. In the afternoon it took me longer to get to sleep as my head was so sore. The pain in my head was so intense that all I could do was focus on it completely, to open it up and prise it apart in my head, to unravel it or find spaces within its dark centre. I fell asleep after about an hour and the same thing happened, my alarm woke me right before granny arrived back with her. The next day I thought I felt a little better but deteriorated quickly and the pain in my head became unbearable. My aunt took her again in the morning and brought her home at 12pm. The days passed in a blur of headache, nausea and my daughter's fleeting smiles as she was passed from auntie to granny through the week. I started feeling weepy and maudlin about the time I was missing with her – this was one of our last weeks of my maternity leave before we went on a family holiday to Italy and I felt as though I hardly saw her. I also had the dawning understanding that this was what it was going to be like when I was back at work, seeing her fleetingly in the morning, the perfunctory feeding, getting ready time before she was whisked off by a cheery relative then returned to me later in the day, older somehow, having had experiences and a life without me. Her growing independence from me was necessary (and I had been beginning to wonder about how the breastfeeding was going to work when I returned to work – I was still feeding on demand, whenever she seemed to want it or when I was at a loss with what to do with her). I would need to try to wean her onto a breakfast, lunch and dinner breastfeeding schedule and then a breakfast and dinner schedule with someone giving her a sippy cup of breast milk at lunchtime. I already knew she was not going to like it. I didn't think I was going to like it either. How could I hand her over her to others all day, every day? Not that I didn't trust them, I did implicitly, it was more that I already felt pre-emptively jealous of the time they were getting with her while I would be in meetings, classes or on the commute. What even is my life anyway now? I felt as though I could not give two hoots about work and could just live these days with my family happily enough. I didn't want to miss out on anything she did, any stages of her growth.

These days of illness were a wake-up call. I couldn't be with her all the time. My husband pointed out that she had had a great week, playing with her cousin Charley, visiting my uncle who played his guitar for her and long walks with her auntie. She might have been fine without me for these blocks of time but I realised that I was less fine without her. The thought of returning to work became like a ball of dread from this week on. As people began to contact me about work-related things in preparation for my return and to check what classes I could do (could I do a 12-hour day my second day back?) I felt panic rising in me. I didn't want this. All the elements of my old life were pushing back in and I already hated it. I liked my new slower, simpler life and the thought of returning to my old role, which had given me so much joy, began to feel like a life-sentence. 'Do you really need to go back to work?' my sister asked. Before, if anyone had asked me if I would give up work after I had children I would have scoffed at the ridiculousness of the idea. Now, however, I would have seriously considered it, had it been financially viable.

I read voraciously throughout my maternity leave. Since 2008 my sister and I have attempted to read 100 books a year. It started off as novels but we both began including others, theory, poetry collections or self-help books, to make the task more manageable. I had never made it to 100, but my sister did twice, in 2011 and 2012. I came closest when I was commuting and the train had no internet; the year of my pregnancy I also read a lot. I wondered if the year of maternity leave would be the year I finally cracked it (and it was – I read 107 books in 2019, then 102 in 2020). The combination of not-much-time to do anything for myself yet periods of enforced stasis due to breastfeeding meant I ended up reading a lot in the first months of her life.

I discovered audiobooks (I didn't count these on my list but they nevertheless provided solace and entertainment when my eyes were simply too tired to perform the action of scanning the page, left to right, and my brain too exhausted to absorb the ideas). I've always been against the idea of e-readers. I don't like reading off a screen and I love the tactility and object-ness of a book. Two well-respected colleagues, when I was going on maternity leave, both encouraged me to get one, for late-night reading in the dark and quick snatches of a book when breastfeeding. One of them, who has two children, pronounced that if she didn't have an e-reader she would not have read a thing for the last five years.

My husband bought me one and I warmed to it at once. I bought a turquoise case with a picture of blossoms on it and immediately enjoyed the ease of using it in darkened rooms and quiet night-time spaces where a reading lamp or light would have been disruptive. True, I did often forget the title of the book I was reading (one of my oft-quotes facts about the evils of e-readers), but I enjoyed the ease of it, the place I had stopped reading kept every time, no awkward weight or strain in my thumb from holding the pages of a book open (by this point De Quervain's Tendonitis was making even this simple task near impossible). It was easy and enjoyable. Why had I resisted for so long?

Usually when going on holiday half of my suitcase was full of books, outfits sacrificed for words, a smart pair of shoes cast aside to squeeze in another tome. On our first trip abroad with our daughter, my slender Kindle slid into a pouch on my hand luggage, no bulk, no worry about the additional weight of the literature I had brought, so easy! And, travelling as we were with a baby, the space this freed up was immediately filled with baby paraphernalia, nappies, wipes, toys and food.

I left her for the first time when she was nine months old. I was working on a research project that meant me spending two nights away from home. In the car on the drive to Perthshire from Glasgow I felt immersed in the green canopy of leaves above us. I realised I hadn't been out of the city since my daughter was born last autumn. I had visited my parents by the sea but had not ventured into the countryside and the lush greenery and green leaves enveloping the road felt like old friends.

When I received the itinerary for the research trip, I noticed the luxury of time in the schedule. Breakfast was at 8.30am, the first session 10.00am till 1.00pm. I was shown to my bedroom, a room used by the nephew of our hosts. The bookshelves were filled with children's books and books on ecology. Louise, our hostess, informed us that the radiator in this room was broken; it was jammed on and there was no knob to turn it off. I volunteered for this room as I'm always cold and it proved to be a toastie haven throughout my time away.

The first night we were there we took a walk by the beaver ponds. I looked at the last fragments of sun reflecting on the still water. I thought, 'this is life, this is it'. Being outdoors and out of the city was like waking up from a dream. The time and space I had during these days felt decadent, a proper holiday from my (m)other life. Although I woke up at 4.00am to feed her, she wasn't there and I fell back into a deep sleep. I awoke again at 6.00am and forced myself to try to get to sleep. I must make the most of this, I thought. When I woke again at 7.00am, I expressed milk while reading *Morning* by Alan Jenkins. His reflections on the sacred time of the morning, the special time when only you are awake and the world seems to sleep were welcome reading matter for my first solo sojourn.

I hadn't realised before we arrived that the daughter of our hosts, Paul and Louise, had a five-month-old baby who lived in the house with their daughter and her composer husband. My shock and delight at meeting their daughter was palpable. She was a smiley and cheerful baby, who didn't sleep much and who had eczema, her delicate face scratched around the hairline. I made a joke about getting my baby fix and asked the rest of the group not to disclose to my daughter that I had been cheating on her with a younger baby.

I asked the new mum if she would like me to hold the baby for a while. I know myself what it is like to be the one always holding, tired arms, sore wrists. I immediately felt the buoyancy of this baby's lightness compared to my daughter's familiar weight. She had a similar baby-ness to her but I noticed the missed intimacy of my own baby's touch. At dinner on the first evening the mother's food arrived first, her daughter was on her lap and she began to eat one-handedly. 'I'll take the baby and you eat' I said, taking the wee one from her. My own meal arrived moments later so, on the first evening without my own baby, the first dinner I could enjoy baby-free, I found myself jiggling this baby in my arms, walking her around the grand dining room showing her the sheep and the grass and the trees outside as her mother ate her dinner.

The payoff for my solitude in these days, for the return to my working life, was that in the morning and the evening and during the lunch break, I would attach myself to my breast pump and empty my breasts of milk. My body didn't know that my daughter and I were apart, my breasts didn't know I wouldn't be feeding her, so still I produced milk. I expressed it and then poured it down the antique sink in the bathroom.

When we were reunited after two days something was broken. Her face when she saw me spasmed as though enraged. My husband said it was because she was trying to smile too hard but I wasn't sure. She had vomited profusely on the drive up so my husband had to hastily strip and change her in a lay-by on the A9. She still smelled of vomit and looked pale, her smiles wan and half-hearted in the evening light. I cuddled into her but something was different, there was a distance. I had left her now.

It was almost like I didn't recognise her as my baby. She looked the same but there was something that had gone awry. My husband gushed over her in a way I hadn't seen him do since the early days. Is that what constant time with her did? Hypnotised you? For me, the spell was broken and as I sat in the back seat of the car, inhaling the pervasive smell of her vomit and stroking her tiny hand I couldn't help but feel a sadness at my decision to leave.

She had never been a sickly baby. When she was very small, her vomit was pale and liquid, inoffensive and almost sweet smelling. 'This spew stinks,' I said to my husband as we hurtled along the motorway in the midsummer light. 'It was a proper big girl spew', he said almost proudly. When I said that it had never smelled so bad, he told me that she had thrown up entire elements of her meal unchewed. Whole bits of macaroni reappeared unscathed as did florets of broccoli and unchewed and undigested chunks of bread. That this had made it down her gullet untouched seemed to amuse him. Before, it was just milk.

CHAPTER 7

The Letdown

I WAS CONTINUALLY engaged in the seemingly magic process of making milk, like a cup that is filled, emptied and replenished. My body became a factory, constantly producing, at work, while I slept and walked and went about my day. This bodily alchemy was juxtaposed with the perfunctory and tedious task of continually expressing milk using a breast pump, hooked up to a device one breast at a time as the milk was extracted from me. I started expressing more for me than for her, terrified of another bout of mastitis which hit when she was two weeks old.

Expressing milk, disassembling the plastic parts of the pump, washing them in hot soapy water then sterilising them for their next use is one of the many tedious, time consuming and sometimes futile aspects of motherhood. These cycles of actions that need done daily (or more than daily) contribute to the feeling of being constantly busy but never getting anything done. These tasks would seem particularly fruitless when, after the labour of preparing the equipment, expressing, storing the milk in the fridge in tiny bottles or writing the date and volume on the top of a plastic bag and putting it in the freezer, she rejected expressed milk outright, her face red with fury and her tiny mouth screaming her indignation at not being at my breast. Different shaped teats with varying degrees of similarity to my nipple gathered rejected in a cupboard and the bottom drawer of the freezer overflowed with frozen sachets of unwanted yellow-tinged milk.

Despite crafting a hands-free pumping method (by cutting two holes into the cup of an old bra to thread the funnel through, liberating me from holding the vacuum to each breast as I expressed), the process itself demanded stasis. Even though I had freed my hands from this task I had to sit still in my rocking chair (not rocking) as the pump tethered me by wires to a nearby socket which provided the pump its power to extract the milk from me. Becoming mother has taught me a lot about slowing down, about stasis, and about the time the body takes to do certain things. Often in the early days when she was feeding I would be impatient, willing her to finish so that I could get up, be active, put on a wash or do some other chore around the house. It began to dawn on me during lengthy feeding sessions that this was the most important thing I could be doing right now. *This is what I'm doing just now.* I am on my strange holiday from my 'normal life' to do exactly this. Once I realised this I started to enjoy it more, to gaze back into her eyes as she looked up at me while feeding. No one has ever looked at me that way before.

When I was visiting my parents who live by the sea, I took my apparatus and expressed milk in their guest room, warning ominously, 'DON'T come in'. As I walked up the stairs

I overheard my dad talking to her in his new cheery voice, his smile audible in the vowels. He referred to me as 'the food machine'. When I objected to this, he said he would not call me it anymore. Another time he called me 'the fuelling station'. I was now the provider of milk, the food machine, the fuelling station, constantly reaching to unhook my nursing bra to release a heavy breast when I saw her feeding cues. I began to feel a growing sense of dread when I had finished feeding her and passed her to an eager relative, when I saw her head begin to move from side to side, rooting about. Hungry again. Back to mum, time for a feed, *hungry again*. Insatiable.

The first suck after the latch, both sharp and relieving. Known as the let-down, the release of milk in the first moments of feeding has other connotations. Women who have miscarriages are said to have 'lost' the baby; an implicit judgement on their mothering is implied through language. There is a sense of blame, a suggested judgement of carelessness – she has lost the baby – she should have been more careful, aware, informed. Of course the loss is felt as a sadness – a grief – and is for reasons outwith anyone's control, but the semantics seem to imply a fault with the mother. The term let-down does correlate with the sense of release of the milk as it is 'let down' from the glands in the breast, however, the idea of being a let-down – a disappointment – lingers around this process like the faint smell of sour milk.

The 'let-down' of milk pre-empts the feeling many women have about breastfeeding, of being a let-down to the baby, not being able to nurture them properly. The first (and only) night in hospital after the birth of my daughter, I was sharing a ward with one other woman, slightly older than me, who had delivered her baby that morning by c-section. Neither of us had names for our babies so we joked that we were the nameless girls ward (the two other beds lay empty). During that first heart-wrenching, fearful night I could hear her whispering to her crying baby over and over again 'I'm sorry, I'm sorry'. 'Poor you having a mother like me'. She was struggling to feed her baby and seemed under-confident in breastfeeding, insisting she must not be producing enough and that her baby was suffering as she couldn't feed her.

While my husband and I were moving as quickly as we could through the various checks and medical processes to allow us home as soon as possible, the woman in the bed diagonally opposite planned on staying another night so she could have support from the midwives before going home with her baby. This feeling of anxiety, of being a let-down, a disappointment, a mother who can't sustain her baby, was palpable from the woman I shared a ward with in the first 24 hours of motherhood. The fear of not being able to feed your baby is very real. In week two, after a full day and night of cluster feeding which left my nipples chapped and painful while worrying constantly that she was not getting enough, I looked at my husband and said tearfully that I understood why women stopped breastfeeding so early.

After one horrible Saturday where I was close to giving up completely, a Sunday morning midwife visit provided the help I needed. She was very matter of fact and conducted what can only be described as a tutorial in breastfeeding. She undermined the advice about feeding lying down which the previous midwife had suggested (due to my daughter's Pavlik harness some positions were impossible) and instead offered hands-on help on how to do it. By hands-on I mean she pierced a white-headed blocked duct in my nipple with a needle and then proceeded to thrust my daughter's open mouth so deeply and fully onto my entire breast I was worried she would suffocate. When I tried the technique of trailing my nipple down the baby's nose then waiting for her to open her mouth wide before shoving the baby's head onto my breast, if I was not forceful enough, she would make me do it again. When my daughter's mouth was not fully open the midwife instructed me to 'wait until she wants it enough' before lunging her head towards my breast. The midwife taught me to rub her tiny hand or stroke the back of her neck and under her chin to stimulate her swallowing and also taught me to count the ratio of gulps like musical time. 1:1 or 2:1 was the best – one suck meaning one gulp while two sucks one gulp was second best. I realised she had been sucking sometimes five or six times for one gulp, a huge amount of work for little reward. While this session left me feeling like I had not been feeding my baby properly until now (thus the cluster feeding – she really *hadn't* been getting enough despite both our efforts), I now had some tools and strategies for feeding that made the process easier and more efficient for both of us.

The painful irony of her beginning to sleep through the night was that my breasts still needed drained at regular intervals. Although she began sleeping for eight or nine hours at a time, my breasts would wake me like time bombs going off at 3.00am, 4.00am. Two months after her birth I noticed that my breasts were becoming uneven. One resembled a grapefruit; the other looked like a bowling ball, engorged and obscene. I began to worry about this imbalance. One breast could be seen bulging out over the top of my bra more than the other and its nipple was larger and longer, my appearance in the mirror looked lopsided and askew. I consulted the internet and was told (like all of the strange pregnancy and post-childbirth transformations of the body) that it is *very common*. I learned that one breast can naturally be more abundant that the other and one breast will frequently produce more milk. I was informed that I may be exacerbating this by feeding more on one side (or perhaps my baby had a preference to one side?) It could be that one side has a stronger let-down reflex or less milk-making tissue. The important thing to remember about breastfeeding, I learned, is that it is SUPPLY AND DEMAND. The more demand there is for milk on one breast, the more that breast will produce. DEMAND = SUPPLY. Again, I began to see my body as a factory, the productivity of one breast going into overdrive to meet the demand of my baby's hungry mouth.

The various internet chatrooms I encountered indicated that the way to overcome this was to 'balance out supply'. The Medela breastfeeding site stated inanely 'All moms are different – and so are breasts!'. I ignored the invitation to join the 'Mom's room' to discuss this but read on. Suggested strategies included: offering my baby the smaller breast first so that she drinks most fully from this; or expressing milk from the smaller breast first, then pumping the other, before returning to the first breast to try to stimulate further production. I was encouraged to massage my breast and remembered the final antenatal class I went to, a breastfeeding workshop, where the midwife handed out round woollen knitted breasts for us to practice massage on. These pink domes could have been mistaken for stuffed tea cosies apart from the brighter pink, brown or beige knitted areola that sat at the top of them, the nipple poking upwards like a cherry on a Belgian bun.

I was told to favour the lower-producing side throughout feeding, nursing frequently on this side to build up supply. There was a caveat: 'be sure not to neglect the higher-producing breast as that could lead to engorgement, plugged ducts, or mastitis'. I realised as I began to try these strategies in the following days, this catch-22 of breastfeeding. By prioritising the lower-producing one to build up supply, the already abundant breast did not get fully drained. If this breast was not fully drained, I felt the warning tingle of the early signs of mastitis, the hard lumps in the breast that indicate a blocked duct or milk in stasis. To avoid this, if I was prioritising breastfeeding on the smaller side then I needed to express the larger one more. But if I did this, was I then encouraging more supply on this side? After all DEMAND = SUPPLY! The circularity of this process and the additional pumping schedule was exhausting. I was told that in three to five days of undertaking these measures my milk supply would balance out. I gave up after two days, resigning myself to lopsided breasts and viewing them as another casualty of pregnancy and child-rearing. I couldn't imagine thinking of them sexually ever again, they are food machines, milk-producers, the part of my body which excreted fluid which for a time my daughter consumed as her only sustenance. I couldn't believe that they would return to their normal size and proportion after breastfeeding, the nipples of both drooping towards the ground like a frown.

When she was three months old I awoke at 4.00am with painful hard breasts but ignored it. I was forced awake at 5.00am with needles stabbing into my chest, my breasts hard and lumpy, like igneous rock, a roadmap of blue swollen veins etched on them. I obediently expressed milk; as usual my left breast was far more bounteous than my right. By 6.00am I was emptied, breasts reduced, milk stored in the fridge ready for a morning bottle. I got my yoga kit ready to put on, removed last night's make up and applied a fresh coat, heated up yesterday's soup and put it in a flask for my husband's lunch, made sandwiches, filled my water bottle and left it poised at the door. I doused the Christmas cake with whisky, a family tradition I'd meant to do at the weekend but had forgotten. At 7.00am I crept upstairs to change into my yoga kit and brush my teeth. I checked on the baby. She was lying eyes wide open in her cot, her hands pressed down by her sides, neck extended like a little tortoise peeking out of its shell. I could smell her nappy from the door. As I neared her cot she beamed at me. I couldn't help but beam back at her as I scooped her up to change her quietly and quickly in the near-dark.

I lay her down on the bed to feed her. If she fed in ten minutes, I thought, I would still have time to de-ice the car, find change for the meter, get changed and go. She fed from my larger breast before I remembered I was supposed to be prioritising the smaller one and flipped on to my other side. If she finished in five minutes, I thought, I could just about make it. Her eyes fluttered closed then just as I thought she was dozing off opened abruptly and widely as her sucking efforts redoubled. As she fed, her small determined fist wavered in the space above her face moving to a rhythm beyond my comprehension. I worried the smaller breast would be empty but she seemed to be satiated and I gingerly removed my nipple from her mouth. I lifted her to my shoulder and gently rubbed her back before putting her back in her cot. Could I make it? I would be a few minutes late but possibly? Her eyes shot open. She smiled and started sucking her hand. Hungry. I lifted her out her cot and placed her back on the bed. I was still wearing only pyjama bottoms with no top so I offered her one exposed breast and she latched onto it, sucking greedily. The time I should have left passed, then the start time of the yoga class too. I imagined them at the studio, on mats, preparing to salute the sun as the sun rises and the sky lightens through the large skylight. I was disappointed, the hours of planning, organising, getting up early, expressing milk, only to be pipped at the post by her need to feed whenever she desires it. She was not working to my schedule; I worked to hers.

I also felt relief. I could stay home, cosy and in bed, with her. I didn't need to go out in the world, to push my body physically at a yoga practice for which I was out of shape. I didn't need to think about where to park, or if I would lactate during the class or if I looked as bad as I thought I looked with my added baby bulk. I didn't need to leave the warm baby haven, I could let the rest of the world get up and go to work and go about their day while I lived in the lawless, timeless, domestic world of child-rearing. A land of unmade beds and warm milk stains on everything. An odour of milk that has been left out of the fridge too long seemed to follow me around for a number of weeks and months. I could smell it in my hair, in my clothes and most pungently in my dampish bras where the nursing pad had either migrated away from the nipple or fallen out altogether as I attempted to choreograph surreptitiously getting my breast out to feed. I stuffed a breast pad under the cushion of my living room couch after it plopped out of my bra when my work colleagues were round to visit.

I thought about my career. I valued it so highly before. What would it mean to take nine months off work? Would I lose my identity when I wasn't working, my feeling of self so bound up in what I do and who I am at work? Would I lose my sense of relevance, of being an agent in the world if I was not existing in the same way in my workplace? I realised while on maternity leave that the flipside of this was that I had a new freedom; that perhaps I was more permitted to be myself in this new role than before I became a mother. While everyone else was getting up early, commuting, working, talking about work, seeing colleagues, going to events, I was gleefully absent from these conventions, restrictions and rules. The languorous and lawless nature of my days proved blissful for someone who has relied so much on structure and busyness. Every night before bed

I used to make myself an hour-by-hour, minute-by-minute plan for the next day: 6.30–7.30 writing; 7.30–8.15 yoga; 8.15–8.45 get ready; 8.45–9.15 commute; 9.15–10.00 class preparation; 10.00–1.00 teaching, 1.00–2.00 lunchtime office hour; 2.00–5.00 teaching; 5.00–6.00 PhD supervision; 6.00–7.00 home and dinner; 7.00–9.00 work on book; 9.00–10.00 bath and get ready for bed. Every minute of every day used to be accounted for, planned and booked with activities, appointments and meetings. After becoming mother, every day stretched before me like a vast motorway, clear of traffic and identifiable features.

In the snatched moments when she was sleeping I wrote furtively. I worked on the academic book I began before I got pregnant and my mind shifted over to a different way of thinking. When her grandparents took her out for a walk, I could become immersed in my work, swallowed whole into my thoughts, trying to piece together the argument I started constructing before I became a mother. Thoughts of another person in another time but familiar enough to attempt to jigsaw together into a whole. I was hit by a tingle in my breast and then a violent pang of missing her. It would happen when she was sleeping, days when I would will her to nap to give us both some respite from the day as it jangled on relentlessly. But then when she would sleep, her soft mouth sucking gently in her dreams, I would miss her. Watching her as I typed to see if the dull clatter of the keys would wake her. Hoping it wouldn't and hoping it would at the same time.

When she woke up, we would dance around the bedroom to *Smells Like Teen Spirit* by Nirvana and I sang along. She would look at my mouth forming the words in the mirror and beam. Her arms and legs would flail as I bopped her about – we were dancing! Blithely, joyously and delirious on the freedom of the moment. *I have nothing I should be doing but this.* I had nothing I would rather be doing than this. My teenage self met my mother self as I relished this moment. Her cheeks were red. She beamed her toothless grin at me, her pink tongue in animation.

I struggled to become immersed in any work, writing or thinking while she was in the house. Even if my husband was watching her downstairs in the living room while I tried to work or sleep, I could sense her gravitational pull. If she cried my traitorous breasts would leak milk, demanding I go to feed her. 'Just ignore us' he would say, 'pretend we are not here and you can get on with things'. This was easy to say and impossible to do as while she was in the house her bodily hold over me was too strong, my mind could not reach the depths of thought it needed to while her tiny presence magnetically drew my physical self to hers. One time he left the house with her so that I could sleep. I must have fallen asleep but I dreamed of her cries coming from outside my bedroom window, as though he had not gone for a walk to the park but had instead stowed her in her pram directly under the window to haunt my sleep.

In another of my dreams there was a large square bath with gold taps. The taps were completely and impossibly submerged as the bath had been running for eight hours. I'm not sure how I knew it had been this specific time but I did. The bath was framed by a large window with dense, jungle-like foliage outside, but beyond this the rest of my memory of the dream is hazy. The large bath, the taps on but impossibly submerged and overflowing. These are the traces I was left with.

When I woke up after this dream, the bedsheet was damp, a large circle of moisture indicating when I had been lying, my breasts leaking, overflowing from me as the water had overflowed in the bath in my dream. *I overflow now*. My body exceeds its boundaries. One night I changed her in the dark, wearing only my underpants. My breasts hung heavy as I reached over her to locate the familiar wipes, nappies and cotton. She let out a sharp cry and I felt the scalding droplets of fluid rush from me. Not as a constant stream but a series of rapid drips, hot on my legs and stomach. At each cry a fresh series of droplets spring forth. I *overflow*. My overflowing is controlled by her and her voice.

At four months old something changed and she went from sleeping through the night to waking every two hours for a feed. 'What fresh hell is this?' I wondered as I returned to the bleary-eyed, headachey and exhausted version of myself from the first month after her birth. She was feeding so much through the night that for the first time in months I didn't need to express milk as soon as I woke up as she had guzzled me dry through the night. In some ways this was liberating as I was no longer shackled to the noisy rhythmic pumping machine which pinned me to my rocking chair every morning. However, while this newfound liberation from the process of expressing, storing, labelling, freezing, washing and sterilising offered some respite, it was replaced with a newfound anxiety that my milk supply was depleting. My husband assured me that breasts are supposed to make the exact amount your baby needs (DEMAND = SUPPLY, remember?) and that I had been overproducing until now, but I couldn't help but feel anxious when I had to go upstairs repeatedly once she was down for the night for 'top-up feeds' that she was still hungry, that I had run out of milk for her and now didn't have enough. I worried I was letting her down.

While breastfeeding, I developed a newfound sweet tooth. I've always preferred savoury flavours, would order a starter and main rather than main and dessert, crisps over cake, but since I began feeding my daughter I found myself craving sweet things, mainly chocolate, first thing in the morning while feeding her. I would have a couple of squares of chocolate with my morning (decaf) coffee or a scliff (my mother's word for a very small slice) of carrot cake left over from guests the day before. Days I was trying to wean myself off this and would make sure there was no chocolate in the house, I would find myself conceding and giving in to my sweet craving, making toast and jam. Once when my daughter was point blank refusing the bottle (one of the many days), I put some of the milk onto the back of my hand and licked it to taste if it was spoiled or had gone bad when I had defrosted it. I was shocked by the sweetness of it, as though my cravings for sweet things was to sweeten my milk to her taste.

My breasts felt emptier, softer, more malleable even before a feed. I wondered if I should start expressing again to try to increase my supply but was anxious that I would express then wouldn't have enough for the next feed. She refused to take breastmilk from a bottle which meant I could never be away from her for more than four hours. Events that seemed far in the future started to creep closer. A weekend away with friends to celebrate a milestone birthday. My sister's hen do. A romantic overnight stay with my husband. All of these attractive events became nightmares of logistics and organisation, ultimately meaning that we couldn't really attend any of them in the way that we had imagined. 'I thought we would be further on by now,' I told my husband as we drove for an hour to attend a two-day weekend party for two hours, before driving an hour back. Four hours, the window of freedom. I was deluded in ever thinking at the outset that we would be able to leave her overnight anywhere, never mind for a full weekend. I had no idea how bound to me she would be, and how close to her I would need to be to sustain her.

In Scotland we celebrate Hogmanay on the last day of the year, 31 December. My husband and I had assumed that by the end of the year we would be able to leave her overnight with grandparents while we went out to celebrate. The four-hour window of freedom dictated otherwise. This Hogmanay was different from previous ones; our daughter was three months old. As the clock showed 11:59pm, instead of standing in a room full of well-dressed people with glasses charged ready to toast in the bells, I was lying on my side in bed, breastfeeding my baby. When I pointed this out to my husband he said, 'It is a fitting end to the year.' It was. To be lying next to the baby who this time last year, unbeknownst to us was already growing inside me, the size of a grain of rice, seemed both so ludicrous and so amazing that I didn't even mind my new anti-social life. I felt my nipple as the stump of a tree whose roots reach deep under the ground. A strong suck from her activated these pathways inside my veins, like threads on a loom they tightened sharply with each draw of her lips. I ended the year at home, snuggled in bed with my two favourite people, quietly kissing my husband at the bells before gently lifting our baby into her cot, ready to wake up together and start a brand new year.

CHAPTER 8

Motherhood

MY MOTHER WAS born in Lennoxtown just outside Glasgow but grew up in Drumoyne, by Govan near the river Clyde. Her father was a welder and as well as working on Scottish icons such as the Forth Road Bridge, he travelled around the world for his work, spending most of the time in South America. There is a black and white photo of him, in his welding gear, with a crew of men. It must have been in the '50s, but it could have been a hundred years ago. Their flat-caps and steel boots, my grandfather's smile gazing out from the past.

My mother was one of five children, the middle child with an older brother and sister and a younger brother and sister. She was the only one to have a big white wedding, she tells me often. She has always been close to her sisters despite her older sister having emigrated to America when she was 17. She and her younger sister have always been close and until my parents moved to the West Coast have consistently lived on the same street. It was a running joke that whenever my mum moved house, her wee sister would appear a few doors down.

My grandmother suffered from ill-health her whole life. My father described her as 'enjoying her ailments' but from what my mother has said, she had quite a hard life. When my mum was small, her mother participated in the trial of a new drug which burned holes in the lining of her stomach. She was so unwell that she couldn't look after her family and my mother and her siblings were taken into care.

My mother often commented on how her own mother was obsessed with cleaning – she cleaned all the time! My mother was disparaging about this, as though she would never be like this. But my overriding impression of my childhood was that my mother was always cleaning. And although I claimed (like my own mother) that I would never be like that, I have found myself obsessive about cleaning (especially when my mother is coming round). Despite our best efforts, my mother became her mother, and I have become mine. And I am glad of it.

My mother, with her hospital corners and lint-rolled linen, immaculately ironed on a Sunday morning, the sweet fresh-washing aroma puffing in exotic clear clouds around her figure standing at the ironing board. Pillowcases facing THIS way and wood polished to perfection, glass surfaces buffed and streak free (I have never achieved such a perfect gleam). A reminder to remove the withered hydrangeas and replace with fresh full blooms. Her conspiratorial tone when she tells me something deliciously SCANDALOUS. Her warmth and soup and insistence that even acquaintances stay for a homemade meal. The soft skin on the inside of her upper arm, the gentlest surface ever touched. When I was wee, I would stroke it in bed in the dark. My daughter now fondles the same place on my body. *Soft*, she says. And history repeats itself.

When I came down in the morning, my mother would be sitting in the kitchen in her pale nightdress with her back to the radiator and a cup of coffee held steaming between her hands. Her knees falling together and drawn close as she tried to warm herself on the chilly mornings. Sometimes I would join her and sit next to her with my back pressed against the radiator too. The hot stripes of metal pierced through even my warmest winter pyjamas and I could manage only a few moments of it before jumping up and going to the cereal cupboard. I always wanted to get the wee breakfast cereals that came in an eight-pack – a mini box for every day. Not only did you get a different cereal every day (and ones mum would never ordinarily buy like Coco Pops or Crunchy Nut Cornflakes) but I loved the decadence of having my very own box to open (then open again as there was a plastic bag inside to keep it fresh). I felt as though I was an adult, in control of my own life, with my individual box, my very own breakfast experience, not to be shared by anyone. 'Waste of money,' my mum said when I lingered meaningfully in the cereal aisle. 'Total waste of money, waste of packaging too'. Then a favourite line, to be used at any shop, fair, jumble sale, market, event or coffee morning by both of my parents at times: 'D'ya think I am made of money?' (The variant 'Do you think money grows on trees?' was thrown in on occasion). I knew my mother was not made of money (and that money did not grow on trees – it was printed in the Royal Mint, I had learned about it at school) but accepted these questions and knew not to respond. I didn't think the wee cereals were a waste of money as quite often I would play with the boxes afterwards, using them for my play kitchen when it was pretend breakfast time. One time I even used the mini cardboard box sides as cardboard to paint on for a picture project we had done in school. When you thought of it that way, they were quite good value (if I recycled them myself afterwards).

The radio was always on in the morning and my mum hummed along, not quite in time with the song. Breakfast was cereal, there was a 'no cooking in the morning' status quo in our house – even on the weekends – although toast spread thickly with margarine was permitted, sometimes with a banana smooshed on top, the yellow flesh merging with the paler yellow glistening layer of spread. When I stayed the night at a friend's house, my eyes grew wide at the jar of Nutella which was on the counter for thickly spreading on heavily buttered toast in the morning. 'D'ya get that every morning?' I had asked my friend tentatively. 'Yeah, if I want it,' she had said nonchalantly. I could not believe it. That night I had told my mum, in the hope that she might consider getting some for our house. 'CHOCOLATE?! FOR BREAKFAST!?'. My mother balked at the very thought and I mooched sheepishly away. I should have known better than to suggest it.

My mum was famous for her 'runny unders'. At the park, all of the mums would push their children on the swings until they were as high as they would go. But my mum would push me higher and higher until the metal chain of the swing was making a horizontal line against the sky when it was flying back to the maximum and forward until you felt like you were going to tip up. Only when the swing was this high would my mum do a runny under. Catching the top edge of the swing, with the tips of her fingers, arms extended up like super-woman, she would grab hold of it and begin to run. Her body doubled over as she reached the centre point and still clutching the black plastic rim of the swing, she would push it forward and up, running and crouching until she was under the swing, still pushing it forward, my legs poking straight ahead, leading the way skyward. My mum would run right under the swing as I screamed with glee as I reached the highest point. The moment of panic as the suspension slackens, before the plummet down and back, a jolt, a breath and a rush of adrenaline. 'Me next Mrs', 'No, me, I want a turn'. The other mums would look at her, ponytail askew, breathless and panting in her tight blue jeans and yellow pumps, standing in front of the swing, watching my giddy descent. 'Give me a minute,' she said. 'D'ya want another one?' 'No thanks, mum.' I wasn't sure if I was going to be able to get off the swing and walk just yet, gravity was pulling me towards the ground and I still clung to the metal chain, my hands marked with the steel and the cold. To be honest, I wasn't sure if runny unders were a bit too high to go on the swings, but I was still proud that my mum would do them. As I tottered over to the grass at the side, I watched my mum pushing another child, a wee boy I didn't recognise. The boy's mum stood at the side wearing a pink parka resting her hand on a buggy with a chubby, red cheeked toddler in it. 'CAREFUL, RYAN' she shouted as he began to giggle with glee. 'It's so high, mum, look how high I am LOOK'. I watched my mum lifting the swing up and down with each push, getting higher and higher before becoming a blurry ball of blue denim and brown jacket as she propelled herself under the swing and broke into a long-strided run at the other side. A younger girl with a runny nose had wandered over to where I was sitting and was absent-mindedly reaching into the long grass and pulling out clumps. 'Who is that?' she asked me, wiping her nose on her sleeve and leaving a silver slug-trail of moisture. 'That's my mum,' I said, and I felt a warm sense of pride through the biting March wind.

I had never realised or comprehended the amount of time and care my mother had put into these early stages of my life. I knew, of course, that she had brought me up and looked after me, but I viewed this in quite an abstract way. Only in becoming mother myself did I fully begin to understand the effort and labour of her role in my life. These first weeks and months and years of her successful care of me I don't remember and have barely thought about, but now I understand her devotion to me when I was a tiny helpless human and I have a newfound appreciation for her and what she did for me.

When I was in my early 20s my parents went to Portugal on holiday. It was their first holiday together alone as a couple since my sister and I had been born. My dad phoned a couple of times and each time he sounded tense and was untalkative. 'I bet they get a divorce when they get back,' I said to my sister upon hanging up on a short and stilted phone conversation with my dad. When they did return, we learned that my mother had been seriously ill, had collapsed in their hotel room and my dad had insisted that they go to the local hospital where she was diagnosed with pneumonia and severe bronchial problems. The Portuguese nurses were encouraging my dad to get us to fly out as it was touch and go as to whether my mother would survive. My dad mentioned nothing and we only found out about this when they returned. She recovered slowly and was off work for a year. I held on to a sense of hurt about this for a long time. I know that they were trying to protect us from the seriousness of the situation, but had she died, we would never have got to see her, we had not even known of her illness until she had past the worst of it. As a parent now, I understand the desire to shield a child from harm, but I still struggle with the idea that had she not lived, we would not have had the choice to see her. This was the first of three serious illnesses my mother has survived. It was only the next year, after she had finally returned to her job as a primary teacher, that she was diagnosed with breast cancer.

A similar pattern. My sister and I were only told of this when it was essential. She should have had a mammogram at 50 but for some reason did not receive an invitation to an appointment until she was 52. There was a discrepancy, but we knew none of this. The first we found out that she had breast cancer was when she got notice of her surgery date and could be shielded from it no longer. She had the choice of having two surgeries, one to remove the cancer and another to have a breast reconstruction. She chose to have them in one, despite her previous illness, despite her heart murmur since birth. She also chose to put the surgery off until after our family holiday to the US to visit her sister, the duration of a month. Madness, I thought, but she did it.

The day of her surgery I was nauseous all day. My dad didn't want us at the hospital but I would have rather been there, close to her for the duration – the surgery ended up lasting nine hours. Instead I was working on developing a performance with a group of peers. I couldn't concentrate and kept thinking 'why am I here?'. To protect can sometimes be to exclude, to leave out. I understand this better now as a mother than I did when I was only a daughter. My mother recovered. She is the strongest woman I know.

CHAPTER 9

(M)Others

FRENCH ARTIST LOUISE Bourgeois, known as the *grandmere* of art, is famed for her giant sculpture of a spider, its eight legs spread over the square in front of the Guggenheim Museum in Bilbao, Spain. Titled *Maman*, French for mother, its arachnid form and tentacular spread of limbs conveys a sense of reaching, of grasping towards something beyond the self as well as providing a sinister kind of protection. I visited an exhibition of Louise Bourgeois' work at the Gallery of Modern Art in Edinburgh. I went with a colleague and friend also with the initials LB (and also with a spider tattoo, which we laughed about as we walked to the exhibition). LB (Louise Bourgeois) said:

> The Spider is an ode to my mother. She was my best friend. Like a spider, my mother was a weaver. My family was in the business of tapestry restoration, and my mother was in charge of the workshop. Like spiders, my mother was very clever. Spiders are friendly presences that eat mosquitoes. We know that mosquitoes spread diseases and are therefore unwanted. So, spiders are helpful and protective, just like my mother.

My mother did dressmaking and design at school and during my childhood was always running us up a skirt or fixing a hem or trying to teach me how to knit. We would go, my mum, sister and I, to Remnant Kings to choose fabric and then she would unsheathe her ancient electric sewing machine to make us a garment (always with a matching scrunchie made from the same fabric; it was the 1990s). I thought this process was fabulous. Selecting the material I wanted (so much choice! So many colours and patterns!); standing at her side while she would thread the needle on the machine, her tongue out in concentration and illuminated by the tiny light in the sewing machine (what technology!); the final swishing of the fabric off the machine, waistband inserted and ta da! A new outfit, chosen by me, made by her. We would use excess fabric to make scrunchies to sell at craft fairs and jumble sales.

She taught me how to knit when I was young and I returned to this in my 20s. I have never moved much beyond items that involve straight lines (scarves, snoods, cushion covers) but I do know how to knit and purl and do moss stitch (my mum's favourite). When I was attending an event in London in my 20s, I sat at the back of the bus with my small bag of knitting on my knee as I traversed the city moving between performance venues. Two young Black girls sat down next to me. 'Who taught you do to that, that's amazing!' one of them said. My knitting itself is of a basic standard, but when they expressed such delight in the constant action I was doing, line by line, stitch by stitch, I did feel as though I had been gifted something amazing. 'My mum taught me when I was wee' I said. How lucky

I have been to have her, showing me things, teaching me things my whole life, almost without me realising until a moment like this, on a bus in a new city, talking to strangers.

When I became pregnant, my mother dusted off her knitting needles and began to knit, purl, knit, purl, knitting with a vengeance for my daughter arriving. She made a beautiful white matinee jacket with matching booties, a bright blue cardigan with red sailboats on each side of the buttons, a full knitted set of tights and cardigan with a matching hat and booties, all in the colours of the sea, and many, many more things. I will keep these for my daughter always, they were made for her, with love and by my mother's hand.

I dressed her in her homemade knitted clothes for starting nursery, I wanted her to feel our connection through the soft garments she wore, a thread between her home life and her new life at nursery untethered from me from ten months old. Nothing could have prepared me for my baby coming home smelling of other people. I had been naïve, assuming she would love nursery because she was a sociable baby at the various classes I took her to. *She loves other babies*, I thought, *she is going to have a great time!* The reality was that it was harder to get her settled than we had thought. Starting nursery was a precursor to me going back to work. This, of course, was inevitable, but I tried to hold on to the last moments of my new life. I spent a whole afternoon shopping for a gift for my PhD student. I thought about what to get her, where I would get it, I picked a card with care and wrote it with thought. I posted handwritten letters to friends overseas. This process felt different from the rushed, hassled, thoughtless way of being in the world I often found myself in previously.

The week before my return to work I heard some home truths from my family. According to my mother, I was breast-feeding through the night more for me than for her. My husband hinted at similar thoughts, that it was me that was dependent on breastfeeding, not her. I was addicted to it. I denied this vehemently but the struggle of going from breastfeeding on demand to restricting her feeds to breakfast, lunch and dinner then simply morning and night was real. I was so used to feeding her at the slightest cue and it was my first port of call for every gripe that it felt unnatural to restrict it in this way.

The first day we were apart was fine, she didn't seem too bothered although was pursing her lips more than usual and latched on eagerly and hungrily for her night-time feed. As the week went on she seemed a little out of sorts, discombobulated, as though something wasn't quite right. I persevered, only feeding her in the morning and in the evening but every fibre of my being felt a strong urge to feed her more. I worried about my milk supply, about her not getting enough nutrients from the diet I was providing her with. Hours of food preparation to make baby lentil soup or leek and potato soup or baby curry and she would reject it, only wanting soft buttery toast, mashed avocado and pre-made Ella's Kitchen purées. It seemed unnatural for me to be away from her, my body rebelled, my breasts hardened in revolt.

I write down things I want to say to you: 'becoming a mother is one of the most profound and meaningful things

I have done in my life'. I change 'a' to 'your'. 'Becoming your mother is one of the most meaningful things I have ever done'. What is life except a search for meaning? The things we weight with significance are the aspects of our lives which give them form, shape, purpose and value. Some of the things that have previously felt the most meaningful and given my life most of its purpose now seem lesser. It's as though the vivid landscape I once saw has been revealed to be an amateur painting, rendered on cardboard, a flimsy theatrical set with nothing behind it, blank space in the wings. This is my real life now. Me and you, you and I.

When considering whether to have children, the state of climate emergency the planet is in was at the forefront of my mind. I had read Naomi Klein's book *This Changes Everything* (which my husband had held in front of my face the morning we found out I was pregnant) in which she outlines the climate crisis and also discusses her own experiences of trying for a baby, miscarriage and IVF. She writes of sitting in a boat in a dead zone of the ocean while having her miscarriage and realising that she is inside an environmental stillbirth, that human actions have caused fertility issues on a planetary scale. That our Earth is becoming an inhospitable environment for life is due to anthropocentric activity. Timothy Morton writes in *Being Ecological* that we may be in an era of mass extinction. Scientists estimate there are only 12 more years in which action can be taken. My daughter will be about to enter her teenage years at this time. Other estimates indicate that by 2050 mass extinction will have occurred and the Earth as we know it will no longer exist. My daughter will be almost my age at this point. What is the world we are leaving for the next generation? What is the environmental legacy of my generation and my parents' generation? How can we bring new life into this uncertain context? What will I say when she asks why more wasn't done to avert this when knowledge of the issue was prevalent? How can I justify my own desire to bring life into the world? I spoke to my mother about my concerns about bringing a baby into this place and time of ecological disaster. She said that before having me, she and my father had similar conversations. They had worried about the threat of nuclear war, been concerned about the life I would have in what seemed like the most uncertain of times. My mother said that perhaps every generation feels like their time is the worst, the most unpredictable, the most chaotic. I think she's right, but I also think that in this particular moment it is true of ours and more true of my daughter's.

CHAPTER 10

One Year On

HER FIRST BIRTHDAY was a disaster. She had been ill in the weeks leading up to it and on the day before her birthday, a Friday, the nursery had phoned me to pick her up early because she had a high fever. When I arrived, she was sleeping awkwardly on one of the nursery staff, her face pink and cheeks warm. The next day, with a house full of guests and a table full of food, we had to take her to A&E as she was so listless. My parents, remembering my sister's meningitis 30 years previously, were distressed. When we got to the hospital, the doctor checked her over and asked about her diet. She thought perhaps she needed more sugar for energy so prescribed some birthday cake when we got back. We gave her some, she perked up and we started her party up again.

When I look back, when I try to make sense of what has happened from her first birthday onwards, I think it was our black cat Lola's death the month after the birthday A&E visit that seemed to mark the start of the bad things happening. When I looked down from the guest room window, I saw Lola in the garden, perched on my daughter's turquoise chair, drinking from a puddle of water that had gathered in the dip of the seat. She was using one paw to scratch the chair as she drank, a gesture I had noticed her using before at her water bowl. She looked up, some noise must have attracted her attention, and as I looked at her I realised that this was probably her last time going outside, of being in our garden. Her heart was failing.

The vet said that we could potentially transfer her to the vet hospital, have her put in a special tank that would help her breathe. She might live another week if we did this but would not be able to leave the hospital. Enough, I said. Her breath was short and noisy. She looked at me. Enough. We had one more night with her at home. It was a Friday night. I wept and held her until it was time to go to sleep. We brought her to our bed and she lay curled by my pillow, a purring inkblot on my white sheets.

I put my hand on her body and I tried to radiate love from my body to hers. As I was falling asleep I could feel her slipping away and the tears I was crying leaked down my face and into my left ear. When I awoke at 3.30am she was still lying next to me, her breath ragged and uneven. I was wracked with sobs, shaking silently trying not to disturb her. We spent time with her and my other three cats in the kitchen in the morning. The light was extraordinary, orange and luminous and Lola sat serenely on top of the microwave, looking out to the garden she had loved so much. I could see her out there still, amongst the lawn, her eyes green and glowing among the strands of grass. I could see her stalking elegantly along the path, sleekit and velvety, her panther-like body close to the ground when she slipped stealthily under the wire into the neighbours' garden.

She sat glowing in the sunlight from the window, purring quietly and constantly until it was time to go. I had bought white roses and they sat in a vase next to the microwave. Black and white, life and death. We had our time with her at home, to say our goodbyes. I took some final pictures of her, and of her and I. I am wearing sunglasses to hide my tears but you can tell from the tenseness in my jaw that I am inconsolable.

When we got to the surgery, the vet left us to say our goodbyes. This felt horrible, obscene, I didn't want it, we had spent our time at home. I was angry, upset, annoyed at the delay. When the vet returned, she explained what would happen when Lola was injected, then surreally pulled out a brochure for urns for her ashes and explained the various pricing options. This too felt obscene, unreal, cruel. The sedative seemed to work and her small feline body relaxed but when injected with the final dose she reanimated, made a sharp dive forward, where we caught her in time. Peaceful, they said, but it was not. It was horrific. As a final insult, when she had passed, the vet put the blanket over her face. I wanted to scream at her, to pull it away. Before she had looked like she was tucked in, going to sleep, and now she looked like a piece of rubbish, ready to be discarded. We left with our empty cat carry case, my face streaming with tears.

I had absentmindedly taken some Ibuprofen without water to relieve my headache and I could feel them in my chest, stuck and hard. The feeling stayed with me for the next three days. Looking back, it was grief that was stuck there, a weighted feeling of sadness lodged in my chest, making it hard to breathe.

She died in October, the day before National Black Cat Day, aged 13, in the month of Halloween, my little witch's cat, the first cat I'd had as my own since she was a kitten, a tiny six weeks old. She had been with me through everything, shared my life with me from my 20s through to approaching 40. She had purred and cuddled me through a cancelled wedding, family illness and bereavement, and many other significant life events. Anyone who has not had pets might think 'it's just a cat', but Lola was a meaningful and important companion throughout my adult life. I loved her and I miss her.

One Monday in November I had to attend a PhD supervision at 5.00pm. This time was not child-friendly and I explained that I would need to leave at 5.30pm in order to pick my daughter up from nursery. When I spoke to my mum, she offered to pick her up – my dad would drive her to the nursery and she would walk home with the baby. It is a 40-minute walk and I was reluctant at first but finally agreed. During the day, I phoned my mum and said that I could pick up our car and collect Autumn as long as my mum was at our house to meet us, enabling me to drive back in for my meeting at five. 'Don't be ridiculous,' she said, 'I want to do it'. After the supervision I walked home part of the way then hopped on the bus. When I returned home something was amiss. All the lights were on in the house. My dad was standing in the hallway holding my daughter who was crying, my mum was in the background, speaking but I couldn't understand what she was saying. I thought she was telling me that Autumn fainted at nursery. I went to my baby and cuddled her. My dad looked ashen. After a few incomprehensible attempts I realised that it was my mum who had fainted. She powerwalked my daughter in her pram the 40 minutes back from nursery, pushed her up the hill to our house, reached the top of the path and then keeled over. My dad, who had been in the living room looking out the window saw it all. Her fall. The pram toppling. Her crumpled figure at the end of the pram. My daughter screaming. He ran outside and went to our neighbours, a retired doctor and his wife, and asked them to call an ambulance.

My mum had come to then passed out again. When she came round a second time she insisted that the ambulance was cancelled. My dad looked worse than her, grey and ill. When my mum went to get changed I cuddled him and he was shaking. He thought he had seen her have a heart attack or stroke and it had affected him badly. My mum was out of sorts but quite dismissive about it: only a faint, must have been the cold, was powerwalking too fast. We all worried that something else was happening, that there was more to this. There was.

She must have got a fright as she went to the doctor that week. My parents rarely go to the doctor so I knew that this must be quite serious for her to venture to the surgery. The doctor sent her for an ECG and other tests at the hospital. After her first appointment she was blasé; the tests looked fine, it was nothing to worry about. I was not convinced, and sure enough, more appointment letters came through and she was due at the Golden Jubilee hospital in Clydebank on 11 December. She was diagnosed with a blocked aortic valve, the main heart valve, which would need open heart surgery to be replaced.

Like a ticking time bomb, I became scared of her being on her own, terrified that something would happen and she would be alone. When she didn't text back immediately my mind went into overdrive picturing scenarios: she has had a heart attack, she is in an ambulance shrieking its way through the wet streets, she is in hospital, unconscious with tubes attached to her chest.

I existed in a perpetual state of anxiety waiting for news of her appointment. The stress of it was unbearable, I felt unable to bear this level of worry. I woke in the night feeling ill with anxiety. I furtively Googled 'aortic valve replacement' under the duvet then stared appalled at the screen. Broken breast-bone, heart stopped, electric shocks to restart the heart, intensive care. It seemed unreal.

She was told to pack a bag in case they did the surgery on her visit to the hospital and my sister and I were on standby to come and visit that day in mid-December. I had warned my work I may have to leave but when I spoke to my mum in the afternoon she was scathing at the progress. 'Waste of time,' she said. When she saw the doctor she was told her surgery could take up to 12 weeks. Three more months of worrying that she was going to have a heart attack at any moment, three more months of stabbing fear when my phone rang. Three more months of her grey face, looking older, her body struggling to keep going. When they were leaving the Jubilee my dad wished the doctor a merry Christmas for when it came. 'Maybe we will see you before that,' the doctor hinted and with that they were out. Sure enough, my mum received notice that she would be going in for surgery on 23 December.

I have always been obsessed with Christmas, not for any religious reasons, but for the decadence of the holiday, the food, time with family and the feeling of it being the most special of occasions. My dad would groan when we would start talking about Christmas in June and menu planning in October. When my sister and I lived together in a flat when we were in our 20s, we watched *The Snowman* before Halloween, so enraptured were we by the festive season. This year, when conversations about arrangements for Christmas became heated, my mum wanting the celebrations to go ahead as usual despite her being in hospital, my aunt (her sister) saying this was ridiculous and how could we all celebrate when she was lying on her own in the ICU, I found myself uttering the unimaginable words 'I don't even care about Christmas'. My husband stockpiled a turkey and pigs in blankets to put in the freezer so we could have a postponed Christmas once she was well enough. I couldn't let myself think about that not happening, and us losing her.

She had open heart surgery two days before Christmas, two surgeries in the end. During the first one, the surgeon managed to go under her breastbone, the least invasive way of conducting the operation. But after being returned to intensive care she had internal bleeding and was promptly wheeled back to theatre where she had a second surgery, this time they had to saw through her breastbone. Two surgeries, two lots of anaesthetic, two sets of antibiotics. My sister and I visited her in intensive care on Christmas Day. She had a full Christmas dinner in the tray in front of her, a cracker poised in anticipation on the side. Her ICU nurse Lindsay became her confidante and friend in the time she spent there. The Irish nurse Sorcha who was with her when we arrived at the ICU on Christmas day joked that she would only get wheeled out of intensive care to her room if she donned her Christmas party hat.

It was a Christmas like no other and the whole festive period felt like a strain, rather than a break, but every time I was feeling sorry for myself about having a dismal time I kept thinking that I would rather have had a rubbish Christmas than have had my mum drop dead of a heart attack in the new year. When the surgeon removed the valve he seemed incredulous that she had been functioning. She opted for a biological replacement, which means she has a pig's valve in her chest now. My sister and I had lots of jokes lined up about this but have not dared utter them yet. The scar on her breastbone looked like a large welt the first day that we visited her in hospital on Christmas Day, but it has faded to a pale line which disappears under the neckline of the v-neck blouses she has always worn and always will. I think of her scars, on her back, where they removed skin to use for her breast reconstruction after her surgery, and on her chest. These are her battle scars, her war wounds, the marks and traces of a survivor. We had Christmas dinner with all the trimmings on 2 February 2020 and it was brilliant.

After she had recovered from breast cancer in 2006, I wanted us to do the Race for Life together to celebrate her beating the cancer. I had done it myself when she had been ill and wanted us to do it together. I thought it would be significant and important for us both to mark her wellness and health. She did it, but she did it for me. I realised that while some women, having gone through something like that, want to fundraise and are active in raising awareness of breast cancer, my mum did not want to do this. Partly it may have been her nature, not wanting to draw attention to herself in that way, but I also think it is because she did not want to see herself in the role of victim or 'survivor'. She never had, throughout the whole thing. It was something that had happened to her, she had recovered, and it was not part of her life anymore. She donated monthly to Cancer Research (and still does) but that was it for her. She wanted to close the door on it, not make it more a part of her identity than it already was. I can see this now, but at the time I couldn't, I just wanted her to celebrate her recovery and to acknowledge it, but she had already begun to shut that part of her life down. The only time I ever saw her upset throughout her own cancer was the day her friend was diagnosed too. That day she wept, but for her friend, not for herself.

I remember standing in her bedroom, now my bedroom, rubbing antiseptic cream into the scar on her back to make sure it did not get infected. It is one of the most intimate moments I have had with my mum as an adult. When I told a friend of mine what was happening with her, he immediately told me I was likely to get breast cancer too and should get tested. This was coming from a place of concern, but at the time I felt like this was a ridiculous thing to say. This was about her *now*, not about me in the future.

I steadied my daughter on my knee with my hand splayed across her chest, holding her while I reached for her beaker of water. It was bedtime and we were together in the almost-dark of her bedroom. I felt shocked at the strong pounding heartbeat I could feel emanating from her, pulsing against the palm of my hand. I thought of her tiny heart throbbing within her chest cavity and I thought of my mother's heart.

As females are born with their eggs already in the womb, my daughter (in egg form) was in me when I was in my mother's womb. Like Russian dolls, she was inside me when I was inside her. There is something about this intimacy and legacy that acts as a thread that sews our bodies together over time. I feel my daughter's heartbeat in my hand, strong and full of life. I think of my mother's heart, weakened, struggling and old (and now bionic). My heart sits between them, the middle ground, the median between one tiny young heart and one old frail one. I struggle to conceptualise mine in the same way I can theirs, it's an enigma, too embedded within me for me to fully understand its shape, health, or role. It is keeping me alive, as theirs are them, I just can't picture my own as clearly.

I had begun to practice yoga regularly again and was feeling the benefits in my new mother-body. It was my body, but different somehow, ribs seeming further out and my pelvis reoriented, the aftermath of the presence of my baby in my womb. My teacher and friend Rosina was guiding me through, helping to find my way back to an embodied practice with her usual care, good humour and encouragement. In January, she was diagnosed with secondary breast cancer having already beaten the disease years previously. She described it as a 'health challenge, not a health crisis' and I believed her. I thought secondary breast cancer meant it was returning a second time, I didn't realise it meant it had spread to other parts of the body. By early February she was dead.

CHAPTER 11

Spring

AS IF IN the space of a moment, we are living a different life. The coronavirus originated in Wuhan, China in January 2020. By February, it had reached Italy and I sat in work meetings discussing concern over students on trips in both places. By March it was in the UK. It was here and the contingency meetings we had been having moved from the certainly hypothetical, the ludicrously over-cautious to the very, very real. Novel coronavirus, COVID-19, was a health crisis on a global scale, the likes of which has not been seen in our lifetimes.

By the end of March 2020, 1,000 people had died in the UK, a jump of 260 in a day. This can't be real, surely? 100,000 in the US. New York is the epicentre of the crisis, cases rising horribly daily. When I hear the figures I think, 'there must be some mistake'. I watch footage of mass graves being filled in New York City, hundreds of wooden coffins side by side in what looks like a landfill, heavy machinery pushing dirt around at the edges.

Boris Johnson, the Prime Minister, is diagnosed with COVID-19 as is the health secretary. Idris Elba has it. Tom Hanks has it. Dyson are trying to engineer ventilators rather than vacuum cleaners in response to the crisis. My friend who works in IVF transferred to virology. No-one wants to have babies, the people I know who are pregnant are anxious. What is happening?

What becomes clear is how woefully underprepared the health service is for something of this scale. Despite the warnings from Wuhan and Italy, the weeks that could have been used for preparation were squandered, theories of 'herd immunity' being bandied about without any sense of what this crisis would need. Protective equipment for frontline health staff, extra hospital beds, more staff trained in intensive care and respiratory specialisms. The Tories had underfunded the health service for years and now the doctors and nurses were bearing the brunt of it. One doctor described it as being 'sent like lambs to the slaughter'. Sites in London's docklands and the ExCel Exhibition Centre are going to be turned into a field hospital. There are rumours that Glasgow's ice-hockey rink will be turned into a makeshift mortuary. What is happening?

In the space of a fortnight, everything changed. Our weekend away at the start of March for my birthday – a night in a hotel in Edinburgh, dinner, drinks, a rare night out to the cinema to see the Korean film *Parasite* (my choice) now seemed unimaginable. How blithe and naïve we were! How gallus! I feel nostalgic for these moments of sharing space with strangers. Never again will we take for granted a walk to the local café, a casual dinner with friends, a wander round the shops, a drink in a cosy, busy pub. Within a fortnight, life as we knew it is gone. The measures were ramped up very quickly – no gatherings of more than 500 people seemed reasonable, then the Scottish football season was cancelled, not too long later murmurings of schools closing, nurseries. After this news, which had many parents wondering how the work they do and the childcare they no longer had would work in practice, our daughter's nursery closed and she was with us all the time. The week after the schools closed, Boris Johnson announced the following measures: no gatherings of more than two people; all pubs, bars and restaurants would close, as well as theatres, gyms, sports centres, and cinemas. The phrase 'lockdown' appeared. No contact outwith the family you live with. No being outside apart from once a day for exercise. No non-essential trips, only for food and medicine. All non-essential shops and services will be closed. Social distancing measures mean you must stay more than two metres away from anyone. Stay at Home. Wash your hands. Shops are decimated of stock: toilet roll, hand sanitiser and pasta the items most in demand. Footage of empty shelves is screened continuously on the evening news.

I follow these developments incredulously. Societal structures which seemed set in stone crumble one by one. The airports are closed. Everything is cancelled. Festivals, gigs, events, weddings (including that of two of my good friends), public transport is reduced, restaurants and bars close their doors (some forever I imagine). The idea of 'bubbles' emerges – of only encountering a limited number of people you live with or need to see for caring responsibilities. The idea of segregating people into bubbles was one of the ways suggested to try to suppress the spread of the virus and limiting contact with others. We were supposed to be going to Seville on a family holiday. Spain goes into lockdown days before we travel. I am secretly relieved. Despite my husband's insistence that the show must go on and that we would have our holiday, I had felt a growing unease about the thought of moving through airports, sitting on a plane for three hours with strangers, not knowing where they had travelled through previously. I could see myself at the airport, hand sanitising furiously while trying to stop my daughter touching every surface in sight.

The conversations we had in the days before they announced the lockdown focused on whether anything would be open if we did go. The things we loved to do – museums, restaurants, wine bars – could all be closed (and they were). Spain had tried to move quickly after seeing what the Italian refusal to give up the Aperitivo had led to. Milan's mayor had donned a t-shirt saying 'Milan never stops', a bravado that the virus would simply not interfere with the Italian way of life. Days later he was soberly reneging on this as the death toll rose sharply. Italians in the north had tried to flee the disease by moving south and had taken it with them, infecting other regions.

As the pandemic spreads across the globe, it brings into sharp focus the way our world works. People, goods, food, products are moving around the planet constantly, objects are handled, then handled again and again at every stage of our globalised trade chain. In the week the news broke, one of my colleagues was in London, another in Australia, myself and others due to travel soon too. People moving, the virus moving with them as contagion spreads.

There is a 'Clap for Carers' event at 8.00pm on Thursday evenings, when everyone opens their windows and doors and claps for the NHS workers who are risking their lives every day to treat ill people. And they were not only risking but losing their lives. Not just older people either – in London, a pharmacist in her 30s and her doctor father died within 24 hours of each other.

Some mornings feel the same as usual, being woken by a gurgling then a cheerful 'HIYA' from the next room. When I go to get her, she smiles and says 'BUBBLES' with a huge grin on her face. Bubbles have become her obsession, her reason for being in the first week of us being home together. I wonder about her earlier ambivalence toward them at baby sensory classes and if this early experience planted the seed for her current fixation. I spent my first team meeting online in the kitchen frantically blowing bubbles to keep her amused before realising I had forgotten to turn my video off. She can't comprehend why we aren't able to do bubbles every minute of every day, and even after lengthy sessions out in the garden, screams when I suggest we put them away and go back inside. 'BUBBLES'. It is a new word and the most used one in these long first days of lockdown.

Many mornings things are normal, 'HIYA', 'BUBBLES', then we go down to the kitchen for toast. The sun streams in the windows as I make it, the clocks have just gone forward and the mornings are brighter, more luminous. I have the radio on, wondering why they are still being allowed to record in a shared studio and listening out for the news on the hour and half hour. These mornings seem normal, banal, only unusual by the lack of time-pressure to be out the door at a particular time for nursery and work. The repetition of the morning routine of breakfast, having alternate showers while one of us watches my daughter then getting her ready, before beginning a day of play, all feels familiar, normal, homely.

When we go out, however, things do not feel normal – quite the opposite. Everything looks the same, but it is not. I find going to the shops fills me with anxiety. As I approach the shopping centre, I can see a queue of people snaking around the side of the supermarket. The queue is long, but mainly because people are standing two metres apart in accordance with the social distancing measures introduced by the government. Many wear masks and gloves. There are security staff at the entrance. I look along to Boots and Home Bargains. They have the same measures in place, one customer out, one in, with oddly spaced queues at their entrances. Masks are not compulsory at this point but I put my scarf over my mouth before entering a store. I can only keep it on for a few minutes as my upper lip gets sweaty with the warmth and anxiety, so I remove it and am immediately paranoid about what I am breathing in. I hold my breath when I have to pass other customers, moving past them as quickly as I can. My gloved hands pile products into my bag then I unpack them at the checkout, before packing them again as fast as I can. Am I less than two metres away from the cashier now? Have I broken social etiquette? Have I put them in danger? Am I in danger? My daughter? I rush home, a 12-pack of toilet rolls jammed into the bottom of the pram. Do I remove the items still wearing gloves? I use antibacterial wipes to wipe down all of the products I have bought. I decide to wash the gloves I had worn and run a wipe over the handle of the pram for good measure. When did this become the new normal? I had been looking forward to going out, I had even worn actual clothes and put earrings in, but I come back shaken, disturbed and anxious. I am glad to return to the safety of my home.

On the first day of April I awake to the news that a boy of 13 with no underlying health problems has died in London, the youngest yet. What is this thing? It is the first April Fool's Day I can remember when there have been no prank news stories. My newsfeed is filled only with coronavirus, analyses of it to date, strategies for coping with it through mindfulness or Zoom-streamed yoga, terrifying stories of spread, and lockdown and death. There is no other news.

I read an article in *The Guardian* which says:

> Every day brings news of developments that, as recently as February, would have felt impossible – the work of years, not mere days. We refresh the news not because of a civic sense that following the news is important, but because so much may have happened since the last refresh. These developments are coming so fast that it's hard to remember just how radical they are.

Airlines are flying empty planes across the Atlantic to protect their slots on these prime sky routes. The climate crisis and the coronavirus crisis seem related, connected, intertwined. Global pollution has fallen and estimates indicate that in China alone, emission reductions since the start of the pandemic have in effect saved the lives of at least 1,400 children under five and nearly 52,000 adults over 70.

Each day unfolds and unravels, this new strange way of being and of being together becoming more familiar with each day. We have not spent so much time together, the three of us, since Callum's two weeks of paternity leave. In the year and a half since we have all been together, all the time, much has happened. We are different people now. But the patterns of time feel familiar, the lawlessness of days and nights and the different intimacy that appears when you can only see each other, and only in your own home, your family space.

A baby who was six weeks old dies of COVID-19, the youngest yet in the UK. I think about what it must be like for mothers with younger babies. I feel for those who are pregnant, the worry of it, the not-knowing of how the virus might affect pregnant women. Both my sister-in-law and my friend are pregnant, simultaneously due in September. They are no longer allowed to do face-to-face midwife appointments, instead having consultations over the phone. The scans have gone ahead but the other hospital appointments and midwife appointments are cancelled. The reassuring touch of a midwife's hands on your belly will not be felt by thousands of women in this time. Many intimate conversations will not be had, questions not asked.

We are missing family a lot. I wonder frequently when I will see my mum and dad again. We speak every day, they are becoming more proficient at FaceTime, but I am missing the long days of hanging out at their house, of them spending time with my daughter and delighting at her antics. I also feel grateful that this has happened when she is 18 months old. She is able to understand things, can engage in activities and crafts. I wonder what this lockdown would have been like at two weeks, two months, ten months. For a very new mother the sense of grief must be harder. The loss of what this time should have been. Visits from family, support from in-laws and new aunties and uncles, food prepared and delivered and heated for you while you are told to sit down. Someone taking the baby from your arms for a while, to give you a break. The imagined maternity leave period as a cycle of baby yoga classes, walks with friends, baby swimming, coffee shops and baby and toddler groups is impossible now. I think of the women who are going through the hardest time, the first weeks when the world is turned on its axis, when there is an existential shift in your understanding of your life and what it is now. I had never imagined myself attending mother and baby groups, the thought left me cold, but actually they provided some solace and comfort in those early days. The power of being with people who were going through the exact same moment was important, the shared experience of new motherhood. I have not maintained contact with any of these women. I saw one mother after classes for a number of months and we went for walks with our buggies, but after I returned to work this stopped and I have not seen any of these mothers since. That doesn't matter somehow, nor does it diminish the time we spent together, warm and friendly chats over tea after baby yoga, sharing types of rejected bottles and comparing teething horror stories.

In the isolation of the first months of motherhood (and it is isolating, no matter how much support you have), these moments shared with other new mothers helped me. After the two-week bubble of paternity leave burst and my husband returned to work, these weekly gatherings and my self-enforced routine of baby classes to get me out the house, to give my day shape and purpose, were invaluable. If the first months of motherhood are isolating under normal circumstances, what must this period of actual isolation, of 'self-isolation' be like for very new mums? I imagine a grief about what might have been (what should have been) and a loneliness that should have been quelled by visitors and family. I also imagine that what I felt at moments, when it was just her and me, after hours of crying with no seeming cause, those feelings of despair and helplessness, will be being felt more keenly by new mothers in these months of lockdown.

When I think back to my maternity leave, the freedom seems almost unimaginable now. Free from work and my usual professional demands, set loose from obligations I might otherwise have had, and, what I now realise was the biggest privilege of all: the freedom to walk around outside with my baby whenever I wanted, to invite others into my home for visits, to stay with family and share the responsibility of her care with those close to me. How blithely I did those things without a second thought. If I have another baby, after this thing is over, I will think differently about those simple pleasures, those basic and banal privileges I didn't even realise I had.

I worry about my mum, about her health, about when I will see her. I worry that although she is not in a large city, she could get infected. I worry that her immune system is compromised after her surgery at Christmas. I worry that this is a respiratory disease and that she almost died of pneumonia and bronchial complications. I worry that if she does get ill, I won't be able to see her. I worry that the last time I saw her, I didn't realise it might be the last time I saw her and didn't make it special or significant enough. I worry that my daughter is missing them. I worry that if we do see them once the lockdown is over, we might still pass something on unknowingly. This is my biggest concern, that we make her ill, and that she might not survive it. As the death toll rises daily, horribly, exponentially, only rarely is there a sense of the person's identity, and only if it is in some way unusual. A very young person, a famous person, a teenager, a baby. But the thousands of people who died are all individuals, they all have families and friends and a whole life's worth of stories and experiences. When the First Minister of Scotland Nicola Sturgeon said, 'we can rebuild the economy, but we can't bring the dead back to life,' she was saying that once people are gone, they are lost, that human life is the most important thing in this moment and we must do everything we can to preserve it. I imagine what losing my mum to coronavirus would be like. For her to be a number on the rising tally, a daily figure on the up. For her to have survived everything else – pneumonia, cancer, heart surgery – and to be lost to this surreal global pandemic feels cruel. The thought of it makes me feel ill.

I begin to feel as though I can't taste things as well as normal. I have heard that loss of taste is a symptom. We all have coughs but it doesn't seem like the right kind of cough. No temperatures. Sore throats in the morning, tiredness. I ache. But we are all run down. I was exhausted before this hit and am now even more tired. I ache from holding, carrying, lifting my daughter so much when I usually would not throughout the day when she is at nursery.

I realise in these first weeks how little I have been home this year. A sliver in the morning, a window with my daughter at teatime then hours mindlessly in front of my computer before collapsing into bed. I enjoy being home. This house is part of me. There are certain sounds and smells and feels to it that are a part of who I am. The creak in the top part of the stairs, an almost musical tone to the four squeaky stairs in succession. I know these noises, I have heard them every morning and evening for most of my life. Now I hear them through the day, up and down, my tread heavier than it has ever been with the weight of my child on my hip.

I start having flashbacks to my earlier life. I go to look at a mirror in the hall which was there for my whole childhood but is no longer. It is as though I am seeking my younger reflection in the glass that isn't there anymore. That version of me doesn't exist anymore, but at the same time she does, held within these walls in various stages of time. I look at my daughter, who my parents tell me is exactly like me at that age. One of the most significant things about having a child is seeing the total, unmediated joy that she has within moments of her own life. The taste of a raspberry, bubbles being blown into the garden outside, the physical sensation of being lifted high into the air. When do we lose this? When do we become self-conscious, self-aware, derisive, anxious? When do we lose this raw joy for life? In these weeks of isolation I reflect a lot on my own life. When I was pregnant I remember understanding my own body differently, listening to it for once. Why do I not always do this? I thought. Why not eat when I am hungry, sleep when I am tired, say no to going somewhere if I don't want to go? Caught up in the busyness of life we can lose sense of what is important. Returning to work after maternity leave, I swore to my husband it was going to be different. 'Work-life balance,' I insisted. No more seeing students after the working day, no more working the weekends, into the small hours to give feedback on assignments handed in late. 'Hmmm, we'll see', he said. I had started off well, leaving on time, not working weekends, but since the start of the new year my role had escalated, I stepped up to do a more senior role as well as my own and my working hours got out of control. I had guilt about this, of course. One particularly busy week I realised on the Friday that my daughter had an infected finger and that her ear was also oozing pus. I have hardly seen her, I thought. I haven't noticed because I am not with her enough to have seen these things. My shame at the pharmacist, two minutes to six, her insistence that I had to take her to the doctor – 'she NEEDS to see a doctor' – I felt her judgement of me as a working mother. Doing all things at once and feeling like I am doing none of them well.

What the first weeks of isolation made me think about was how busy we are all the time and how little time we spend reflecting on it. It made me question my life. I could see a simpler life; I was living it. A quiet life at home, with my husband and child. We focus on what we are going to eat, what activities we will do to get us through the day. I make a meal planner and an activity planner – colour coded for each activity (garden, toys, outside, home baking, arts and crafts). I come up with art projects for us, a woodland scene, an under the sea sticker project, a weather chart. We draw a rainbow and put it up in our window like the many other families in our area with children who can no longer socialise. When we are out for our daily exercise I point them out to my daughter. The huge one painted directly onto the glass which spans all three panels of a bay window. The A4 one with 'be happy' written in childlike handwriting underneath. We see more every day that we go out. 'Meeno', she says when she sees them and I realise this is her saying 'rainbow'.

What can this moment teach us? To lead a simpler life? To get rid of all the extraneous activity that we do? To have what we need and no more? My old life seems extravagant now, wasteful. I portion up a pot of soup to ensure it does us all for two days. I count the chicken breasts in the pack and plan how to stretch them out over multiple meals. I save my daughter's breakfast scraps for lunch. I am becoming more frugal, more careful, more considered in my use of things. Why could I not do this before? I thought I was but I wasn't really. Is this what it will take for everyone to change their behavior? It saddens me to think that we can only make these changes to our lifestyles, drastic, sweeping changes, when it affects humans directly. We can't (won't) do it for the climate crisis, for the mass extinction that we are witnessing unfurl. We are so selfish, I think. And I know that I am selfish. Because I don't want this to affect me directly. I don't want to lose my mum to this. Or my dad. Or anyone close to me or my husband. Or my friends. That is selfish. I can make the changes, stay home, wash my hands, do conference calls with my child sucking on my cheek, work in the evening tired from playing 'bouncy bouncy' all day (our newly invented lockdown game), but I don't want the grief, the devastation of losing a parent. But people will suffer this. And people are, every day, the death toll ticking up and up and up.

Every day I am aware of what everyone else is doing when they are 'working from home'. Walks with the dog, baking sourdough bread, gardening, cooking. I don't want to feel resentful but I am. Working two jobs from home plus looking after a very energetic toddler made me feel that all of this 'spare' time that everyone had suddenly found was exclusive to those who didn't have children. I long for the windows of time, the idea that hobbies might actually return to my way of life. Many people are on furlough and are making the most of enforced time off work while having some financial support. I take a week of annual leave. I had booked a week off anyway as we were supposed to be going to Seville. This week I am able to spend time with my daughter and as it is my husband's first week working from home he was able to acclimatise to this with me doing most of the childcare. I had a good week with her, I didn't feel like I had been off, but with my out-of-office email response on I at least felt like I was not on call all the time for Zoom and Teams meetings as I had been. I also have two research deadlines, which I meet late at night, then feel absolutely exhausted and drained after they are submitted.

During the second weekend of lockdown, I finally manage to do some yoga. My daughter has an epic, unheard-of nap of two and a quarter hours which allowed me to fit in an ashtanga practice. Since my yoga teacher Rosina passed away in February I have struggled to practice. April 2020 was supposed to be her memorial, the Sunday of the second lockdown weekend. When she passed away, I told my husband that it didn't feel real, that I hadn't come to terms with it and that it would only be at her memorial that it would finally sink in. I was not projecting this: the same thing had happened to me when my friend, performance artist Adrian Howells, took his own life in 2014. I was numb when I heard, disbelieving. A mistake, an error, I kept thinking. Or an accident. He had got his tooth fixed the day before, surely that was not the action of a man about to end his life? Or maybe it was, a tying up of loose ends. I have known people who have passed away before (mainly older relatives), but suicide is harder, it cuts deeper, the inevitable questioning of what could have been done differently to change the course of what happened. After the most recent conversation we had, why had I not been in touch more? The last time I saw him was in January of 2014, I met him while crossing the road between Hope Street and Renfrew Street in Glasgow. I was leaving the Citizen M hotel having returned from Thailand the night before, late, and having stayed in the hotel with my (now) husband when my flight landed into Glasgow Airport as I was living on the West Coast of Scotland at the time. I saw Adrian across the street but as I was walking towards him, my suitcase in tow, my shoe fell off and I was caught in the crossroads fumbling with my case and my shoe while hopping around with one socked foot exposed, panicking the traffic lights were about to change. Adrian waited for me patiently on the other side, but when I reached him I felt bashful, ashamed at my clumsy fumbling and having lost a shoe, and also shy from having not seen him in a number of months. He seemed upbeat, but the subtext of the conversation was that his mum was very ill, she was struggling and he had been spending a lot of time at home with her in Sittingbourne, in Kent, his childhood home. I had never met his mother but I felt as though I knew her as she had featured prominently, along with other members of his family, in video material which he had used as part of his show *An Audience with Adrienne* for which I had acted as production manager numerous times over the years. We had performed the show at the Saltmarket in 2006 as part of the Glasgay festival (a celebration of queer culture based in Glasgow), then taken the show to the Edinburgh Festival in 2007, performing two shows a day as part of a British Council run, then to the International European Theatre Meeting (IETM) in 2010. I knew the work well, having watched the performance hundreds of times, and in doing this, knew Adrian intimately as the work was autobiographical and invited the audience to share stories too.

Adrian's mother had been a force in the films, fiercely protective and proud of her son, warm, yet at times cutting his dad off from saying things that perhaps he would have liked to have said. When I saw Adrian on this weekday morning in January, he seemed well but his anxiety about his mother was palpable. We hugged in the street, saying we would meet for coffee soon. That was the last time I saw him. I pored over that conversation again and again, and our subsequent text messages, looking for clues, for signs I should have read differently. The guilt and regret of a friend's suicide is a particularly difficult thing to accept. It is not simply death, a feeling of something out of your hands, but instead a sense that you did not do enough, an empty space which is filled with questions and shame and chastisement. It was only at Adrian's memorial, a grand affair at the University of Glasgow chapel (Adrian had completed a fellowship in the Theatre Studies department in 2009) that my numbness dissolved and I spent the whole beautiful ceremony wracked with sobs, receiving concerned looks from partners of friends. I surprised myself at the depth of my grief on that day, that I was unable to control it, and that I had not been able to access or accept it before that day.

Rosina's death was a shock in a different way. She was such a force that after her passing I kept expecting to see her in my building where she taught staff yoga as well as students of voice and performance. It sounds strange to say, but I had been looking forward to her memorial, if only as a chance to be around the people who knew her best. Rosina and I shared many communities, firstly, at the Arlington Baths Club where she ran her yoga company. Then, the dance and performance community around Glasgow and beyond. Rosina's influence was wide and deep, everyone taught by her felt special, because that is what she did and her capacity as a teacher, mentor and friend instilled a confidence in my ability that I did not have. But gradually, as she believed I could do it, I began to believe too. Her unwavering support and confidence in what I was able to achieve with my body pushed me beyond my self-imposed limits. I grieve not only for her, but for the part of me that was lost when she died, the part of me that had just started to believe in myself again.

I also feel relieved that she did not see the COVID-19 crisis. I feel relieved that her health was not affected by it, glad her business did not go under because of it, happy that she did not have to witness the community she had worked so hard to build be forced physically apart. I know that if she had been here, she would have been such a positive energy in keeping the practice going, in whatever way she could have, but I also felt that my own memories of physically sharing that beautiful loft space in the Arlington, with a glass roof where you could see the clouds drift and the seagulls from the Clyde swooping and soaring, remain intact. My memories of her body, pressed against mine as she adjusted me, are still very present. The night she died I could physically feel her body on mine, an intimacy that is not afforded to many. I felt devastated that her memorial was not going ahead due to the coronavirus measures as I was longing to grieve with friends, colleagues and students who all knew and respected her. I was also afraid that if I didn't have that moment, I wouldn't fully accept that she is gone, that I would feel as though she was away somewhere, in Crete where she went every summer, to teach and holiday (she built a house there), and would continue in this distracted, busy limbo of unacceptance.

I miss her as a person, her energy, her positivity, but I also miss the way I felt about myself when I was around her. Like things were possible. That I could achieve the impossible. That my body, which I had variously loathed, ignored and abused over the years could be strong and powerful and make me feel really, really good. My husband had said that he didn't mind getting up early for me to go to yoga on a Wednesday morning as it put me in such a good mood for the rest of the day. I confided to him after Rosina's passing that it was partly the yoga practice, but largely being with Rosina, that would set me up for the day so well.

When I practice yoga on my own, the day before her memorial would have been, I remember her advice. I hear her words and instructions in each posture. I remember her laugh, loud and sudden, a burst of fabulous joy in amongst the measured instruction she delivered. As I raise my legs up into headstand, I remember the feel of her body standing next to me as I attempt this. Her words, once I had achieved the pose without her touching me: 'Laura, I am leaving you'. At this, my body would hover for a few moments longer, then crumple. I did not need any physical support in this pose but needed the psychological support of her standing near me to be able to do it. At home, and sometimes in the studio, I would practice against a wall.

I did not need a wall, I never touched it, or Rosina as she stood beside me, but without a presence behind me I could not do it. 'Courage, Laura' she whispered to me one time, and I knew this is what I was needing, this is what her presence gave me that I lacked in myself. This day in early April, I feel her there, I lift my legs, one by one to the ceiling and I invert myself into headstand. I don't wobble. As I breathe into the pose, I focus on feeling the strength in my arms as she taught me. I breathe in and out 15 times and have a moment when I feel I could do more, then her voice in my ear again, my guide, saying as she had so many times before, 'that's enough for today'.

My cousin received a letter saying he should not leave his house for 12 weeks. He lives alone and recovered from stage-four Non-Hodgkin's lymphoma two years ago and is therefore high risk. I worry about people who live alone, particularly if they are being told not to go outside at all. To wake up every morning alone, to spend the days, like many other days, within a set number of walls, with the same kinds of tasks to be done, with no human contact apart from via a screen. What will this do to our children who are learning to only be with their mum and their dad? Who are missing grandparents, nursery friends, nursery workers, aunties, uncles, cousins, playdates? What will it do to their sense of socialisation as they grow older? I worry for those who are really alone, those elderly or high-risk people who will not see another human for months. How sad for them, how sad for us. This is a lonely time.

I write every day throughout lockdown. I am not sure if any of it is very good or is simply a way for me to document my thoughts and the things that are happening. Events are moving at such a pace that I am trying to catch moments before they slip through my fingers. I write more in these weeks than I have in months, an attempt to put down in words the strange shifting feelings I have about what is happening. At times, intense joy at a moment with my daughter, her laugh, delight at the game we have invented and are playing, at other times a sharp feeling of loss, despair, grief and an out-of-body experience that I am living a simulation of a life or having an extraordinarily real-seeming dream. One that feels familiar from disaster movies but without the membrane of the screen to make it feel safe.

The second day of yoga, I am more rusty. My muscles complain about yesterday's stretching and I seem to be stiffer. I know that if I am able to make time to do this every day it will get easier, but this morning it is harder, I huff and puff, my knees lowering to the floor at moments for respite. I try not to be disappointed, it is a practice, I tell myself, but I feel old today, tired and unhealthy. I will feel differently soon, I tell myself, and after a while I can feel my body slipping more easily into the postures, more fluidly transitioning from one asana to the next. I think of Rosina's words: 'joy is a choice'.

Rosina's online memorial is painfully hard. I miss the people I would have been with, the physical contact, the inevitable moving, hugging, dancing that would have happened. We are invited to plant something for Rosina either on the day of the memorial or the day after, which would have been her birthday. I leave it until the day after, until my daughter is in bed. I wait till dusk, noticing that the moon is full. I go to plant a tulip bulb in my front garden. I associate tulips with Rosina as she often used them in images of the studio and they remind me of her. I am pretty sure it is the wrong time of year to be planting this bulb but I think of Rosina's spirit, of how she made anything possible, and I whisper her name as I push the bulb deep into the earth. It is almost completely dark now, I can just see the soil on my hands. I wipe it on my trousers and stand for a moment, breathing in the evening air. Everything is as it was, but is also completely altered.

The same night I plant a tulip for Rosina, it is announced that Prime Minister Boris Johnson is in intensive care for coronavirus symptoms. My husband tells me that he had been boasting about visiting a hospital and shaking hands with patients a few weeks ago. He has had symptoms for ten days. His fiancé also has it and is pregnant. My husband thinks he is arrogant and that he believed he wouldn't get it. I wonder if the nurses treating him are resentful for the way in which his party has eroded the NHS, for the fact he cheered when a pay rise for nurses was rejected in the House of Commons. Whatever your opinion on Johnson, he is still currently in charge of the country and the news that he is in intensive care unsettles me. Intensive care is where you go when your body can't function on its own, I tell my husband, it is when you need round the clock care. I think of my mum at Christmas, in intensive care while recovering from her surgery. Johnson is not on a ventilator yet, reports say, but I have been reading articles that say 66–80 per cent of people (depending on which article) die after they go on ventilators. What if I wake up in the morning to the news that the Prime Minister has died of coronavirus? The moments of the news and what is happening in the world feeling surreal are occurring frequently, the strange out-of-body sensation I have is not only due to tiredness; it is my mind struggling to compute the vertiginous shifts in what is happening and the speed at which this crisis is unfolding.

A few days later, the Prime Minister is moved out of intensive care. I feel relieved. I had a strong sense that the crisis pitch to which things had escalated made his imminent death feel like it was the next inevitable part of the unfolding drama. We are invited to clap for Boris in the same way communities have been clapping for carers on Thursday evenings, but there does not seem to be the same enthusiasm to clap for the Prime Minister, certainly in Scotland. My hope is that having been so ill, he might have a newfound respect for the NHS and want to invest more heavily in it after this coronavirus pandemic is under control. Instead, I feel as though he is let off the hook for his dubious policies and handling of the crisis as people are relieved that he didn't die. I feel uneasy watching vast conference spaces in Glasgow and London being converted into hospitals, the huge cavernous spaces being divided into tiny cubicles to hold thousands of ill people. Surely not all of these beds will be filled? With the death toll up to nearly 1,000 a day now, and the peak still forecast to be weeks away, it is suggested that even these vast, make-shift hospitals (the Nightingale in London was completed in nine days), will not be sufficient for those who will get ill. It is nightmarish.

My days with my daughter feel a world apart from what is happening in the news. I immerse myself in our games, in the times when I am with her, alternating childcare with my husband, I want to give her my full attention, all of me. This is not always possible and there are days when I am on conference calls in the kitchen while she plays, trying to concentrate on what is being said on my screen to then realise she has been scribbling on a cupboard. But for the most part I try to remain present with her. It also makes me feel good, this one-on-one time with her in our little mother-daughter world. She is learning so much and her speech is developing quickly. I don't know if this is a notable shift since the lockdowns, or if we have just become more finely attuned to her almost-language as we are spending so much more time with her. I have pangs of regret in moments where she does something that she has learned at nursery that I haven't seen her do before. It makes me think that I have been missing so much. At night, trying to get her to sleep, she looks at me deadpan, then does a comical 'shhhh' with her finger to her mouth. She put her hands together, places them by her head and tilts it, then pretends to snore. I try not to laugh as I don't want to encourage play at bedtime but realise that they must do this at nursery, at nap times. Now in the mornings, when I am up with her first, when she asks for daddy, I tell her he is sleeping and she does her sleeping mimes and pretend snores.

My two lives – my on-screen work life (as it is now) and my embodied, felt, intimate home life caring for my daughter – feel more disparate than ever, despite the fact that I am doing my work from home. I am missing sharing spaces with colleagues and students, I am missing the live element of teaching.

It is hard to have the same connection with people working entirely online. I think about how the only people I see, touch, smell and share space with are my daughter and husband. I miss my mum and dad, my sister, my in-laws, my friends. The not-knowing of how long this will go on for is also hard. Wuhan in China, where the virus is believed to have started, has just lifted its lockdown and travel ban after two months. We are three weeks in, but reports are already announcing that the UK looks to be the worst hit of all the European countries, with some estimates saying that our death toll will exceed that of Spain, Italy and France combined. There is critique of the government approach, the initial 'herd immunity' approach – that we should all get it to build immunity (with many thousands of people dying) – then the slow move to shutting schools and businesses which potentially allowed the virus to spread before the lockdown.

The mid-April day which should have been my best friend's wedding is beautiful. A lovely day for it, I think in the morning. We should have travelled to Islay, where her family is from, by ferry on Good Friday. We spent a lot of our teenage years visiting Islay in the summer holidays, to stay in her gran's old house, owned by her dad since her death. The name of the house is written on a plaque outside surrounded by a collection of shells and sea urchins. The house name is Gaelic for 'peace' and it is situated in a quiet and secluded place, just outside of the village of Port Charlotte on the West side of the island. We used to joke about how it was enforced relaxation as there was nothing to do on Islay (this was before I discovered whisky, of course – there are eight distilleries on the island and a peaty Islay single malt is my favourite whisky now). We used to sleep all the time there, whether it was the sea air or our teenage want, I am not sure. We stopped going on our trips to Islay, in our 20s, but then started visiting again with gusto in our 30s. My friend would spend every Easter and summer holiday from her job as a primary teacher in Islay with her immediate family and her partner and had a lot of family still living on the island to visit.

The decision for her to get married on Islay was easy, it was a special place for her and her family and we were all excited to be there for her special day. The last time we were on Islay was the August of the previous year when I was eight months pregnant. It was my husband's first time visiting the island and we stayed in my friend's family home. We bought a bottle of Laphroaig Quarter Cask, my favourite whisky, and made a last-minute video for our child-to-be at a different distillery in the final moments of our trip before we got on the ferry. We both signed and dated the bottle and planned to give it to our daughter on her 18th birthday. It sits, just now, in the glass-fronted cabinet in our living room, biding its time.

We had been looking forward to returning and were disappointed that the swathe of cancellations included this island trip. However, our disappointment was nothing compared to how my friend must have felt, to have had to make the decision to cancel the wedding as it became apparent that group gatherings were not going to be possible. For what is a wedding but a happy gathering to celebrate the love of two people?

I tell my husband how grateful I am that we are okay. We have challenges at work and a huge amount of juggling to do with our jobs and child, but no major life events had to be cancelled. Our jobs were relatively secure. We have had our wedding, our hen and stag weekends, our honeymoon. We are okay. We are very lucky. We are lucky my mum had her surgery before Christmas. We are lucky that my family members with cancer are over their treatment and were not reliant on hospital visits. My sister's honeymoon has been cancelled. My other friend's wedding and the hen weekend in Belfast looked dubious. Another friend texts on what would have been the morning of the wedding, Good Friday, to tell me his son had been born, 20 days early. He was able to be at the hospital for the birth but is banned from visiting. They are hoping his partner will get home soon but in the meantime she is on her own, post-c-section, with her premature baby. We are so, so, lucky.

I hear two bees buzzing above my head as I play in the garden with my daughter. The sun beats down on my bare arms, the first time it has been warm enough this year to brave being outside without a jumper. I can hear the children next door playing in their garden. Two bikes whizz by unseen along the back lane. The sky is unendingly blue. My daughter blethers to herself as she moves stones from one part of the path into the flowerbed. She picks a mixture of purple and white stones up either with her hand or her fluorescent green spade, puts them into the orange bucket, and when a certain volume has been achieved, picks up the bucket, waddles over to the foliage, squats, and tips the stone into the plants. The colour of her spade is the same as a belt I had when I was younger. On a family trip to a log cabin in Callander, I remember a horse tried to eat my belt which we all found hilarious (but I also found quite terrifying). 'It must have thought it was grass because it was green,' my mum said. This made perfect sense to my childhood brain and I trotted this out every time I told the story – 'the horse thought it was grass because it was green!' Only now, as a parent, do I see this for what it was, my mum helping me to connect colours and objects, and even though the nauseating, fluorescent green was nothing like grass, she was trying to help me learn, to understand colours and the way they connect with objects and concepts in the world. I recognise this now as I do this continually with my daughter: your jumper is blue like the sky; your bucket is orange like an orange; your teddy is yellow like a banana. As she potters around, her task of moving the stones around the garden so vital it cannot be stopped or paused for any reason, she speaks her almost language, 'daddy, papa, bubbles, apple, papa apple, cheese, shoes, bubbles, ta, daddy'. There is something comforting about listening to her pre-speech. The word which most commonly recurs is 'bubbles' and she spots these everywhere.

She can't say m, so *mum* or *mummy* is impossible. My husband points out that she calls me 'Bissy'. Daddy and papa have been perfectly annunciated for a while, but mummy and gran (which comes out as a guttural ch sound – like in loch) are not there yet. I joke with my students on the first day back (online) that I hope she is not going to start calling me 'Bissell'. The first day of online teaching after the spring break is hard,

I dress up, put perfume on, as though I am going to be with people face-to-face. I think it helps. I sweat a lot, alone in my room, my laptop balanced on a yoga brick sitting on a paint pot, precariously.

I tell my husband I don't want things to go back to normal. In fact, this situation has made me realise how ridiculous 'normal' was. Many things that were deemed unfixable have been resolved overnight. People wouldn't stop flying to reduce emissions to slow climate change, but now many flights are grounded and airlines are going bust. We couldn't stop there being homeless people on the street, but now this has been solved with hotels and hostels made available. Do we want to go back to the previous nightmarish normal? In terms of our lives, thinking of the rush, the stress, the early morning starts, the getting dressed and fed and out the door by 8am, working all day, no lunch break, stuck in traffic at rush hour to get to nursery, flying home, my daughter crying, bags thrown in the hallway, jackets off, dinner out the fridge, heated in the microwave, answering emails on my phone while she eats, shoveling my own dinner down to get it out the way, quick play, bathtime on my own, bedtime on my own while my husband works late. She is down by 8.30pm, and I go back on my laptop to work until I can do no more and collapse into bed. No time at home, no time to watch the plants grow, noticing when they need watered or fed. During lockdown, my foliage has never been healthier. I am getting the little jobs done, a cupboard cleared out here, a drawer emptied there. It is cathartic. Finally moving a small way down the endless list of tasks that I cannot ever seem to get to feels really good. Time with my child is joyful. I am going to miss her after the lockdown, I am going to miss the quality of time, our closeness.

First thing in the morning, she grins at me. 'Daddy', she says. The first word out her mouth when she awakes from her nap, 'Daddy'. They are falling in love with each other, I can see it. Their shared routines, their walks, the bubble machine he bought her, their silly games, their bumping down the stairs. When I walk downstairs and see them cuddling on the couch after her nap, I have a pang of love so strong it takes my breath away. My family. We will look back on this time as precious. I don't want it to end.

Of course, that is one strong, clear feeling I have about this situation. That a simpler life is possible. That all I need is home, family, food, the small comforts and pleasures that have come to punctuate our days. Watering the plants together, a shared pot of coffee in the morning, the ritual of a glass of wine towards the end of the day. I am taking extraordinary, ridiculous pleasure in these things.

The other feeling I have is a deep and primal dread. A fear that rocks me to my core. A feeling so toxic that when I go to the supermarket and have to go through the process of waiting in line, social distancing, wearing gloves, Perspex barriers around the tills, tape on the floor, I feel as though I am going to have a panic attack. The most banal of tasks – grocery shopping – has become an impossible mission, a dreaded and feared set of interactions with others. It is as though I can sense the contagion in the air. I hint that I am finding being out in the world stressful to my husband but don't reveal the extent of my dizzying horror at what the outside world has become. I don't leave the house for days on end apart from to potter round our garden. I feel fine. So many of my anxieties have dissipated now that I am home all the time. My perpetual anxiety about having left an appliance on when I leave the house, the gas hob, the iron, a candle, no longer haunts me. I no longer worry about the house being clean in case someone pops around unannounced. I don't worry about people I don't know ringing the bell or dropping parcels as this is not allowed. My fear of flying and dread of future flights has dissipated as we cannot travel anywhere. I can have the washing machine and tumble drier on without obsessing about them combusting while no one is home as we are always home. I don't need to worry if I have everything packed in my daughter's bag as we never go anywhere. I don't worry about hygiene in restaurants or if she will be disruptive to other diners. I cook everything from scratch, I wash my hands, I stay home. We are not free but I feel liberated from many social anxieties and general anxieties about modern life. I am putting on weight, I don't care, as no one can see me. I need my eyebrows waxed, I pluck them myself. I need a manicure and pedicure, I do it myself. I need work done in the house and garden, I do it myself. I am becoming a self-sufficient person who is only now realising the wastefulness of my previous life. I am not spending money. What do I spend money on usually? Eating out? Activities for my daughter? Shopping? I can't even think of what I usually fritter my money on, but unusually, during the lockdown, my account sits at the same amount for weeks, untouched. I am not going anywhere, therefore I am not spending money. If only I had realised this I could have sorted out my finances a long time ago. Doing stuff = money. I have learned a valuable lesson about the extraneous and non-essential elements of my life.

After a month, the cracks are beginning to show. We are still very much enjoying time with our daughter, but the relentless schedule of work, childcare and domestic duties is taking its toll. I remember pre-lockdown thinking if one small thing happened, if our daughter was sick one day, or if I had an issue at work that kept me late, the precarity of our arrangements would be exposed. I felt that in my role, to take time off at all seemed impossible, and only if it was to tend to a sick child. Of course I would do it, but I would feel anxiety about breaking from our very rigid schedule. In lockdown, everything has fallen away, all childcare support and all semblance of a work/life distinction. The nursery has been closed since March and our generous support from grandparents is impossible due to the government restrictions. They are missing her terribly and we wonder if it would be okay to meet in a park at a distance (it is not). I fantasise about driving her along the A82, round the Rest and Be Thankful, through the Argyll forest to Dunoon, to have an illicit encounter with my parents on the beach outside their house. I won't do this (of course) but I do long to see them, and for them to see her. I also feel very strongly that I want to see the sea again. As well as distance from my parents, our enclosure in one environment has started to grate on me. I am aware also, that we are privileged in this situation. We have a nice home, lots of space, a small front and back garden which get the sun at various times of the day. Our daughter has a sandpit donated to us by the neighbours, we have a bubble machine, a paddling pool, should the weather be kind enough. We are the lucky ones. The fourth weekend of lockdown we do everything we did the previous one. A walk to Victoria Park on my daughter's new trike, a barbecue in the sun with wine and nice food. But where last weekend I relished this, felt so lucky and grateful for this strange, government-imposed holiday from our usual way of being, this weekend I feel an angst, a restlessness, a sense of unease that I can't seem to shake despite the good weather.

In the park, a police van crawls along the path to the pond. It parks, and two police people get out and begin approaching those who are lying sunbathing on the grass. No one is having a party, or a barbecue or is in a large group, but many are sitting on benches or the grass, in twos, enjoying the sun. 'Are they moving them on?' I ask my husband. 'I think so,' he replies. Our daughter runs towards the pond shouting 'cack, cack, cack!' and brandishing her beaker as the birds beat a hasty retreat.

We walk as a family through the park, resplendent with spring blossoms. My daughter fell on her face in the front garden on Friday skinning her head and nose. At the park, running wildly in a summery jumpsuit, she falls and skins her knee. 'Uh oh', she says. She looks like she has been in the wars, her new life of being outside a lot apparent on her body, skinned knees, dirty nails from digging in the soil in the front garden, trying the occasional mouthful. She pulls a face. 'Uh oh' she says, her tongue black with dirt and I lift her into my arms and into the kitchen to try to scoop the remainder of the soil from her mouth. She tastes the yellow petals of the yellow poppies – 'cack cack!' – she associates the yellow with the pictures of ducklings in her books. A purple lavender head is also popped in her mouth then quickly fished out. She seems drawn to taste the colours of the garden, when at the dinner table anything fresh – bright red strawberries, green broccoli, orange tangerines – are rejected as she demands only beige food.

I have never felt so connected to my home. When my daughter and I are tidying the front garden, she wanders over to a nook where the red sandstone of the house meets the hedge which separates our front garden from our neighbours'. The last panel of the bay window leans forward into the garden creating a small area between the hedge and the house which feels enclosed and private. I have a flashback to being in the garden, around age four, collecting fallen rose petals from the other side of the window, walking along the stone path in front of the window, then arriving in this enclosure to create perfumes mashing the rose petals into a cup of water with a stick. I used to pour the mixture into old shampoo and conditioner bottles – the little travel ones that my dad used to bring home from hotels when he was travelling for work – to create a set of perfumes and potions. I would keep these on a shelf in my room before the water would become too brown and stagnant to be aesthetically pleasing and then I would begin the process again. As she potters around in this area, stick in hand, I can see that its intimacy appeals to her too. What will she get up to in there? I wonder, as I watch her toddle around, exploring.

I notice all the things my friend Scarlet in Australia has given me that live in my home – a spoon holder; my soup pot (it was her pot which she left to me when she returned to Australia); some white and blue dishes she bought me in Bristol; a blue and white ornament with boats on it that she brought me as my something blue when she came over as a surprise a few days before my wedding; essential oils and other trinkets she has sent me over the years. I photograph these things and send them to her, a montage of memories provoked by a more intense noticing of my space than usual.

The vocabulary of papa, bubble, cracker, daddy, Gruffalo expands almost every day. Fox, socks, bat, hat, shoes, wow, yeah. She likes to match things. 'Socks,' she will say, pointing at my feet, then 'socks!', triumphantly pointing at hers. Recognition, connection, I can see her trying to make sense of the world. She holds her Peppa Pig phone to her ear. 'Hello. Yeah? Bye.' We laugh as this mimesis is obviously of us, of our work phone calls. She points to the photos in her room. One of my husband in the delivery room, blue scrubs, very young-looking, holding her minutes after she is born. 'Daddy'. The next one is of her, a few weeks old, her tiny head resting on my husband's fist like she is thinking. 'Papa!'. 'No', I say, 'that isn't papa, it's you'. I point to her. She points to herself. It is the first time I have seen her acknowledge an understanding of her self-ness. 'Me'. She points. 'That is me'. The final photo is of her and I, in recovery after surgery, her tiny in my arms. I am smiling at the camera. 'Mummy,' I say. But she can't or won't say Mummy. Sometimes I am 'bissy', but Mummy is yet to come.

It is becoming clearer and clearer how badly wrong the government approach has been. As care home figures begin to be counted, the number of coronavirus deaths leaps to over 26,000. I read the figure incredulously. How can this be? I was lecturing about a performance company Blast Theory's performance parade in 2019 which marked the worst flu pandemic in history in 1919, which killed 20,000 people in Philadelphia alone. A devastating loss for one city. That was the deadliest pandemic the world had seen, until now. As I speak to my class about this work, I feel a sense of unease and uncanniness that we are now living through one of the events that will change the world, that will be marked, analysed and historicised.

CHAPTER 12

Summer

BY THE START of May, the novelty of lockdown has worn off. When I speak to my sister there is an underlying sadness I can tell we both feel about the prospect of more weeks of this. The things we are missing are not so much the activities, the meals out or trips, it is simply being in a room with family members. Hugging, being close, being able to read their body language and feel their presence. Screens are good for keeping in touch, but the interaction is always at a distance, incomplete and poorer for it.

My cousin who is shielding has not seen another human for seven weeks. My in-laws have not seen our daughter for nine weeks as they were self-isolating in the weeks before the lockdown. My husband says newspaper sales are up. The roads seem busier, the park is heavily populated with people enjoying the weather. The only signifiers that this is not a normal spring are the pale blue facemasks people are wearing and the distance between walkers who are clearly not from the same household. I have stopped going to shops, it was making me too anxious. But overall, I am less worried than I was at earlier stages. I am less obsessed with hand sanitiser and washing my hands because I am always home. I live with my husband and daughter in our own germ bubble.

My daughter is obsessed with bubbles, we blow bubbles in the garden every day. She whispers the word under her breath when they appear, hushed tones as though to reflect the magnitude of the magic of them. They *are* magic, I begin to realise, or if not magic, then certainly extraordinary. What are bubbles? My breath, pushed into liquid, which is suspended in air, blown by the wind, carried away until it meets a surface or object which punctures the svelte liquid casing. Bubbles are a visual illustration of the way our atmosphere works, they show us liquid, air, gravity. These are the scientific elements that they depict. But in their petroleum-sheened, spherical perfection, they also offer a lens through which to view the world, a rainbow-esque diffraction through which whatever is on the other side of them is visible, yet transformed. As we blow bubbles every day I think about how extraordinary they are, how light and free. How simple, yet complex. I too begin to whisper 'bubbles' with reverence as they float and glide upwards from our small square patch of garden, exceeding our boundaries and beginning to roam up and beyond towards the sky.

I have cylindrical shapes bulging from every jacket pocket, a stash of bubbles for every occasion, wherever we might go. On our second week of lockdown in the park I am blowing them for our daughter to chase when my husband says, 'maybe this isn't a good idea'. I realise he means in light of coronavirus. Bubbles, so harmless and childlike and fun, all of a sudden become beautiful bombs of my toxic breath, my germs encapsulated in a perfect sphere, drifting in the air ready to pop and spray my trapped breath all over an innocent bystander. Instantly horrified, I stop. This is what it is doing, it is changing everything. Not changing the activity or the action itself but shifting the meaning of the thing to something darker, more dangerous and deadly. I hate it for this, for ruining these things.

The death toll rises. The government announces that social distancing could go on for some time and the lockdown is confirmed for another three weeks. All of the milestone dates pass, pangs of what could have been but also, perhaps, a relief. The stag weekend in Lisbon my husband should have been on, my weekend in Copenhagen with my girlfriends. I would have been flying out a day later than everyone else then leaving a day early to accommodate work commitments, but I would still have been there. The relief as the days and weeks begin to fly by is also the acknowledgement that I had overbooked myself in these months, I had over-committed to work, external examining trips, research projects and social events and occasions. It was looking almost impossible to do everything, and it was. One thing I want to remember after this is over is the way in which this simpler life, this move away from my usual kind of busy, has exposed the myth of constant busyness as success. What is success? Being so tired and stressed from career building that the weekends are about recovery and bracing for another week? That the constant work commitments mean that I see my daughter for a few hours a day and perform perfunctory tasks, clothes on, teeth brushed, breakfast, dinner, nappy change, bath, bedtime. Where is our time to know each other? Where is our time to be friends? Where is our time to explore together to find things out, to notice things? Bubbles, I think. Where is the time for bubbles?

My daughter becomes obsessed with the car. She points to it outside the window, 'vroom, vroom'. When outside, she pulls me towards it. 'VROOM VROOM'. I realise she wants to go in the car. I strap her in and she sits happily in her car seat, playing with a toy phone with the car door open while I potter about in the garden. In the days that follow her obsession deepens. She wants the car to move. My husband starts driving her around the block. Every time we go outside, she wants to go in the car. He starts parking the car down the street so that it is not visible from our front room window to try to stop her seeing it and wanting to go in the car. My husband suggests that maybe this is her trying to tell us that she wants to go somewhere or do something different. The week that she becomes fixated with the car is the seventh week of lockdown. At the start of the week she is wild, we realise that perhaps she too is starting to get fed up with only seeing us. Her world has become smaller again, more like in the beginning, when it was the three of us. Before grandparent days of childcare, or nursery, it was us, and this is where we are again. Does this feel like a regression for her? How will this affect her? Will it disrupt her socialisation with other babies and toddlers? I try not to worry about it too much, instead trying to make sure she has the best time she can with us. We read, do crafts, bake, plant seeds, go for walks down our street where she roars 'HIYA' at every person we meet. She becomes like a celebrity on our road, waving energetically to her public – the families sitting out in their gardens in the warm weather. The summery weather continues, we water the plants together, go to the park at the weekends, barbecue most Saturdays. It is a simple, ideal kind of life. A neighbour says she is enjoying it, then she says, 'that is disgusting to say, isn't it, when so many people are dying'.

Watching back footage of Boris Johnson boasting about shaking hands with people who had coronavirus in hospital seems like watching a parody. It is like he is setting up a gag in which the punchline is him ending up in intensive care due to his arrogance and exceptionalism. But the joke isn't funny. Because while Boris was in the 50 per cent of people who leave the ICU alive, the other 50 per cent were not so lucky. Or were not such strong fighters, if you follow the Prime Minister's rhetoric. Those that have died, they didn't fight hard enough, did not have enough of the Blitz spirit that has been so inappropriately transposed onto this pandemic. Harking back to British wartime mantras, an era of Dame Vera Lynn and rationing and, yes, a sense of collective effort against an enemy (at the time), but this wartime throwback can only go so far. We are not fighting a war with other humans. This 'enemy' is invisible. If you believe many of the articles that focus on the environmental and ecological elements of the development of the virus and how it jumped from animals to humans, it is an enemy of our own making. It is largely indiscriminate in that it can affect anyone (although studies are showing that people of colour and poorer people are most likely to die from it).

The idea that we can 'fight' and 'beat' it (in 12 weeks Johnson initially claimed, although he has become quieter on that front in recent briefings) is not only false, but dangerous. Framing it in this way puts the emphasis on the person, on their personal 'battle' with it, and if they die, well.... The Prime Minister beat it! Be like Boris.

The new messaging that came out from Downing Street after seven weeks is to 'stay alert' rather than 'stay home'. The ambiguity of this might seem unfocused and unintentionally vague, but I have no doubt that the government is relying on the freedom of interpretation of this that will mean that many people who are now being forced back to work will die. After this announcement, images of the London transport system, busy with morning commuters returning to work, the majority without face masks, shocks me. Packed buses, tube platforms crowded with people, the official advice being to 'try not to face other people'.

The number of transport workers who have died of the virus is second only to health care professionals. Bus drivers, taxi drivers, railway workers, all in constant contact with large volumes of the public, but without the same expectation or demand for personal protective equipment. The transport worker in London who was spat on while working and died of COVID-19 two weeks later. Spitting can be seen as attempted murder now. It is. Bodily fluids are deadly, the virus unseen but in the air, both literally and metaphorically.

This is why 'stay alert' seems like such a nonsensical message. Stay alert implies that if I have my eyes peeled on my daily walk I will notice the virus lurking on a lamppost where someone has recently rested a germ-laden hand. If I am alert enough I will avoid it, and if not, then it is my fault. If I get really ill and end up in intensive care, or if I die, I did not fight hard enough to beat it. Johnson did it, so it is possible. You are just not trying hard enough. The idea that being alert to an invisible and imperceptible virus which can be completely asymptomatic in one person and be deadly to another is ludicrous. It is so ridiculous that it cannot be unintentional. The government wants people to feel like they can go back to work so that the economy can pick up, even if it means putting hundreds of thousands of lives at risk.

I read an article which claims that one in 400 people in England have the virus right now. First Minister Nicola Sturgeon stays with the 'stay at home' message and is scathing about Downing Street's message and its vagueness. *The Guardian* run an article inviting people to Scotland to holiday on the picturesque island of Lewis now the restrictions have eased. 'Not in Scotland' is the vehement message from our press.

Three weeks into the month of May, eight weeks into the lockdown, it is our third wedding anniversary. We had talked about trying to take the day off together, to do something nice as a family. As the date approached, our diaries had both filled up so we decided we would try to finish at 5.00pm to have the early evening as a family then the night together. As the day ramped up my diary was even fuller than it should have been. Two meetings I had forgotten about appeared meaning that I was in Zoom meetings from 9–5. My head was pounding by the end of it and when I finally finished my last phone meeting at 5.30pm we sat in the garden and had a glass of fizz with our daughter playing with her chalk on the path. On our first anniversary I had wanted us to write a letter to each other every year we were married. We wrote beautiful letters the first year, then last year we were so busy with our daughter and did not get round to doing it. We missed it this year too. It was 9.00pm before we sat down to dinner on the couch.

The First Minister has announced a staged plan to get us out of lockdown. From next Thursday we will be allowed to meet another person from a different household in an open space outdoors. She encourages us not to go too far, not to travel a distance where you will have to use their toilet. I think of travelling to mum and dad's, of how we could meet them on the beach or in their garden. I know my mum really wants to see my daughter and I hope that I don't get annoyed if she tries to go too near her or bend the rules for social distancing. I haven't seen them for so long. It is the longest time in my daughter's life that she has not seen her grandparents or aunties or anyone apart from my husband and me. My in-laws drop off a hamper for our wedding anniversary, leaving it on our doorstep. We wave from the door and they stand at the end of the path in the rain. My daughter stares at them blankly. Not sure. Finally, she smiles at her papa and we go back inside.

I speak to my friend in Berlin. She says that measures have eased, that restaurants are opening but with 1.5 metres between tables and everyone wearing masks. She has started dating someone. I wonder what coronavirus has done to the world of online dating. Berlin has not had many deaths despite its size. Throughout she has been meeting friends in parks for socially distanced walks and drinking outdoors as this is legal in Germany. It has been different here. We have not seen anyone.

The weather has changed, it is raining all the time. We have some cosy days in the house, making pancakes and watching movies but I feel relieved that the weather has turned months in rather than days or weeks. It is harder to find things to do with a toddler when going outside is not an option. My daughter is still joyful, chatty, blethering away in her own language, the odd word perceptible to us. Gruffalo, biscuit, cracker, daddy, bubbles. Her mantras follow us around the house. 'One more,' she says with her finger raised. She does this at bedtime for cuddles. 'One more.' I worry she does not understand what this means as I always say *one more* then can't resist scooping her up again to inhale her bath-clean baby skin.

But she is not a baby anymore. The day after our anniversary she turns 20 months old. She is long, tall, confident in her movements, becoming bolder by the day. She climbs everything. She seems to love to be stood or sat where it is most perilous. The kitchen countertop, the kitchen table, she balances teetering on the arm of a couch before throwing herself forward into the cushions.

The end of May, ten weeks into lockdown. The restrictions have been eased. You are now able to meet family members in open spaces (like parks and gardens). You are advised not to go into their houses and to bring your own plate. The instructions seem strangely framed, an unlikely mix of consideration and caveats which make for an unsettling and confusing feeling. Bizarre elements seem highlighted with little explanation. Don't travel so far that you will need to use their toilet; no gatherings of more than six people but police will not be able to access houses and gardens to check this. I speak to my friend in Australia on her way home from her first dinner with friends. She is elated but anxious. It was so lovely to see people, she said, but now she has concerns about how not everyone is following the protocols to the same standards. She worries she should not see the people she has been seeing now she has mingled.

My in-laws come over for a barbecue. I feel a similar ambiguity – I am excited to see them, but I worry about it too. My husband's gran had a bad fall and my mother-in-law has been seeing her. What if we pass something on? We barbecue, the paddling pool makes an appearance for the first time this year, my daughter is a little strange with them at first but before long is shouting 'GRANNY' and 'PAPA' and cooking up pretend sausages delightedly on the toy barbecue they have brought her as a gift. She loves it and her plastic steaks and faux burgers sizzle away as we catch up with my husband's parents and my father-in-law fixes our back gate which has been broken for months. It has been three months since we have seen them and who knows how long until we see my parents.

At the end of May, George Floyd was murdered by four police officers in Minneapolis. He did not resist arrest but a policeman kneeled on his neck while he said, 'I can't breathe.' The world had been in lockdown for three months. Studies show that people of colour are more likely to die from the virus – in the UK they could be four times more likely to die if they contract it. George Floyd's death provoked a huge upswelling in anti-racist feeling. As though the months in isolation had been a pressure cooker, after this act of brutality (one of many, but this instance was significant in an urgent and new way), the world erupted into anti-racist protests and demonstrations. Crowds gathered in defiance of the guidelines. In Athens, people wore masks with the words 'I can't breathe' written on them. George Floyd's lack of breath in his dying moments and the psyche of a global population at the mercy of a deadly respiratory disease become conflated. George's breath is the breath of the world and his death marked a significant shift in how racist violence was understood.

There is a day, a Saturday, when I crumble. I feel physically ill from stress, my mood is so low that I can barely drag myself out of bed at 6.00am to get my daughter her breakfast. When I am with her she scratches me, claws at my face and pulls my hair. I weep and she looks at me shocked before reaching her tiny arms towards me to cuddle me. I hold her close but moments later she is clawing at my hair again. 'Please don't hurt Mummy'. I cry into her neck as I try to extract myself from her tiny sweaty fingers.

I feel so low, a depression so dark and awful has descended on me. I can't do anything. I have so much to do but I can't, I just can't. I go to bed. Try to sleep then feverishly write some emails in the hope that dealing with some of the chaos of things to do in my mind will help me to relax, to be able to invite sleep in. It doesn't, my mind is full, the to-do list too long, my body feeling so feeble and incapable to even lift my head. I realise I am not coping. I am aware there is something wrong. My head is sore, I feel as though I have a hangover but it isn't that, it is something worse, something more insidious, I feel as though things are coming to a head. I long for sleep and finally it comes. When I wake up I feel the same. It hasn't lifted and I feel despair.

As lockdown eases, some commentators argue that the government strategy is still to pursue herd immunity due to the increasing number of cases. The death rate at the start of July 2020 is 137 in one day – higher than when we went into lockdown, but the government carries on regardless with the easing of measures. Images of Bournemouth beach with the headline that the UK is the 'jackass of the world' circulate. The first weekend in July, outdoor seating areas in pubs and restaurants open and pictures of Soho in London show people crammed shoulder to shoulder to each other between pubs with a speckling of High Vis police jackets amidst them trying to disperse them. I feel a sense of rising panic every day. I watch the crowds gathering at Black Lives Matter protests, huge gatherings in Hyde Park then in Scotland, at Holyrood and Glasgow Green. The protests and not the policies will be seen as the cause. People will die for what they believe, I think. People have commented on the wave of protests happening globally in response to the Black Lives Matter movement, but one newspaper headline says it is 'Parties, Not Protests' which will be responsible for any spike in cases.

By July, Scotland has had a series of consecutive days with no deaths recorded. Progress is being made and First Minister Nicola Sturgeon appeals to people not to move too quickly and to continue to take care as beer gardens open in Scotland on 6 July 2020. It has become clear from the footage down south that inebriated people cannot socially distance, and radio reports plead with the public not to overload the health service with drunken accidents as people let loose after four months of lockdown.

My mother-in-law has hand-made us masks, a blue and green patchwork one for me with French text on it, and a mini-one in a blue balloon pattern for my daughter. She is surprisingly co-operative about wearing the mask, docile even. *Munny*, she says in a muffled voice from under her mask pointing to my masked face. She wants to wear hers when I have mine on, and when it falls off in the shop she insists that I hook it behind her ears as we continue down the aisle. After a walk with my sister in Kelvingrove Park, we all use hand sanitiser before we leave. My daughter insists on holding the near empty bottle then on the half hour journey home she compulsively sanitises. Is this what coronavirus toddlers are learning?

I have been nauseous, exhausted and hormonal and I wonder if I am pregnant. We go to the chemist. My daughter stands patiently at the entrance while I put her backpack and harness on. I have my mask on and I ask her if she wants to wear hers too. 'Yeah,' she says. I hook the straps over her tiny ears and she looks up at me expectantly, ready to go. She follows the arrows on the floor of Boots to navigate the aisles. She has learned all this already I think, this is part of her growing up, as normal to her as learning how to put her coat or shoes on before going outside. To me it feels strange, horrifying at times, that this is how we function now. I am completely accepting of the safety measures around masks and agree with it totally (unlike many in the US who are making mask-wearing a matter of their individual liberties), but I can't escape the fact that it makes me feel like I am living in a parallel dystopian universe.

I am not pregnant. The nausea, exhaustion and moods seem to be a side effect of lockdown. I am both relieved and sad. I would welcome the focus that a new baby would bring me, the shift away from work and a sense of rebalancing, but I am also aware of the physical stress on top of the emotional stress that I have been under for these months. Becoming mother in a pandemic? It would not be the perfect time, I think. But is there ever one?

My husband leaves to go to play tennis. As the front door closes and I hear the car engine start up on the street outside I have a feeling of panic. Can I parent on my own? I feel inexplicably bereft. He is only gone for an hour but I realise how unusual it is for us to be apart now. Even in busy weeks where it feels like we hardly see each other, both working beyond midnight then collapsing into bed, he is still a presence, another human who brings life to this space we inhabit. His departure from our house made me feel newly vulnerable. What will the lasting effects of this be?

On her first day back at nursery we book to go for lunch at one of the new beer gardens that have popped up in response to the COVID-19 crisis. The Cranside Kitchen is situated next to the Rotunda by the Clyde, a cylindrical building which has a doppelganger at the opposite side of the river. The Cranside Kitchen is so called as it sits next to the Finnieston Crane, a large crane which looms over the Clyde as a relic and reminder of the time when Glasgow was the 'second city' of Great Britain and was world-renowned for ship building. My husband jokes that not many people will have booked the day off to celebrate their child going back to nursery. It wasn't that I wanted to celebrate, as her return to full-time daycare felt bittersweet, but instead that I was hungry for some time together as a couple, for us to be out together talking and laughing in a way that had not been possible since the start of lockdown. It sounds counter-intuitive when you are spending so much time under the same roof as someone to say you missed them, but the work and life demands on us during lockdown meant that whole days would pass with only the perfunctory passing of our daughter between us, between meetings, between meals, with little more than a few words. Lockdown was taking its toll on both of our energy levels and mental health, but as a couple, it was hard for things to feel as special or as carefree as before, simply because they weren't.

We didn't plan to end up in a pub on the first day they reopened but that is what happened. There was an illicit thrill in crossing the threshold into the dark basement pub on a sunny day. Most of the seats outside were taken and only one other table inside had people at it. We slipped into the dark green leather booth and looked around at the familiar wood panelling and log fire of one of our favourite pubs. We had to leave our details with the bar staff (unmasked) but apart from that it felt pretty much as it had been. The first sip of beer from a glass pint was heavenly, and the second no less enjoyable. Was this okay? As few more people came in as the day turned colder. Was this safe? I tried not to let my anxieties around the virus ruin what had been a special day.

We are preparing to see my parents for the first time, my mum has been shielding since March and in total we have not seen them for four months, the longest I have ever gone without seeing my parents apart from when I lived in Australia. I have my daughter's bag packed a week in advance, I discount seeing anyone else in the days before we travel as I am terrified of transferring germs to my mum when we arrive. They will not social distance from my daughter, but my sister and I discuss how we will not hug our parents when we arrive. This will be strange but feels prudent. My parents have been preparing their home and garden for their granddaughter's arrival for weeks. They have made new paths through the undergrowth, fresh features in the garden for her to explore and enjoy. As though she is royalty, the extensive preparations have been long in the planning and execution.

We travel to Dunoon on 12 July 2020, a Sunday. We are nervous about the travel, although by driving and taking the car ferry we will have no contact with anyone. We still wear our masks on the boat for when I roll my window down a fraction to post out the ticket to the collector, also masked. The nervousness is about seeing my mum, about how it will be after all this time, about her health, about our visit being too much for her, or, most terrifyingly, making her ill. The thought that we could be transporting germs to her, oblivious carriers of an unseen virus makes me almost cancel. But we go.

We are reunited on their driveway, my mum runs out the house and my dad arrives a moment later. My daughter is unusually shy, smiles at first then bawls when papa scoops her up for a cuddle. The weather is glorious, we lunch outside, we are all smiling a lot, so happy to see each other after all this time. My dad tells me that while he has been looking forward to our visit, my mum has been really, really excited to see us. My mum hears this and confesses that there was one night she was so excited that she could not sleep.

Their house on the West Bay in Dunoon has a sweeping garden which leads to a gate directly on to the beach. They bought the house for the garden really, and it is spectacular, a large oval lawn surrounded by shrubs magnificent in colour and texture. The garden has been transformed into a playground for my daughter. There are gnomes on the ground and colourful butterflies in the trees. A plank of wood has been attached to a tree by rope to create a dubious-looking swing. My dad has placed shells on the stumps of trees to help with her counting, one shell on the first stump, two on the second and so on. There is a sign that indicates this is her garden and he has put a sign on his boat with her name on it, the small vessel placed on the grass so that it can be manually rocked to enthusiastic choruses of 'Row, Row, Row Your Boat'.

Her favourite part is a small table under a rhododendron with a glass jar with stones and marbles and jewels in it.

There is also the tiniest plastic strawberry, fluorescent pink, within the blues and whites of the stones. My daughter spends hours with my mum tipping out the jar onto the table then carefully placing each item back in the jar before beginning again. The strawberry is always first to be returned as the most tiny and precious of the jar's contents. We spend the day outside, breathing the sea air and being guided by my daughter as she explores the garden. We remain socially distant – my dad has strategically placed the seats in the garden at a two-metre distance – but we can feel the closeness and joy of being together again.

My mum's scar on her chest is a pale whisper of what it was before. She looks strong and healthy and she scoops her grandchild up to look over the sea wall. I look at them, my mother holding my daughter, gazing out to sea, both gleeful and windswept, laughing and free as the sun breaks through the cloud.

CHAPTER 13

Autumn

IN THE AUTUMN months, when the lockdown restrictions started to intensify and the freedoms we had enjoyed in July and August evaporated, my mum started working on a project she had been talking about since before my daughter was born. When I was two, my parents bought a hand-crafted doll's house. It had been built in the 1950s and was a beautiful two-storey house with a pair of front panels which opened up to reveal a range of rooms. With this fourth wall removed, each room was exposed in intricate detail – and it was detailed – the person who had made it (for his daughter we think) had hand crafted fireplaces, a staircase and banister, tiny light fixtures and (the most amazing part of all) real working lightbulbs that came on and illuminated the house when you plugged it in to the mains and pressed a switch on the side of the house. My mum and sister and I had 'renovated' the doll's house when my sister was six and I was ten. We had gone to a specialist shop to buy tiny carpets and wallpaper with miniature patterns on it, made new matching lampshades out of the wallpaper and tried to make the doll's house as similar to our house as we could. We even tried to put some of the furniture in, as though it was a simulacrum of our own home, the tiny playmobile people standing in for ourselves. My sister and I fashioned minuscule foodstuffs to enhance the reality of the kitchen – little bacon and eggs made out of Fimo to go in the frying pan that was the size of a button. A bowl of fruit with a banana the size of a nail clipping and microscopic grapes. It wasn't just playing with the doll's house that we loved; it was the creation of it, the crafting of various everyday objects that would make it seem more like our 'real' house. When my dad bought a flatpack conservatory to be built on to the side of our home, we used kitchen roll holders and sheets of acetate (sourced from my dad's college's stash for the overhead projector) to construct our own version of the glass extension that had appeared adjacent to our house. We even mixed oats with white paint to give a pebble-dash effect to the exterior.

While I was pregnant, my mum started talking about getting an electrician in to sort out the lights of the doll's house so it would be ready for my daughter. I reassured her that there was plenty of time, as she was yet to be born, and even when she did appear, would not immediately be demanding the use of a well-lit doll's house. My mum brought it up regularly, that she wanted to renovate the doll's house, that she needed to 'get a man in' to sort out the lights (although I was dubious that anyone would want to take on such a tiny job) and that she was going to buy new decorations and spruce up the tired doll's house. This seemed to take on a new urgency in the second phase of lockdown. She started to say that it had to be ready for Christmas (although if we would even be able to see each other then was uncertain). And so from September to December my mum cleaned and glued and painted and re-carpeted the doll's house as we had together as a family 25 years before. She even managed to get the lights fixed and was delighted with the result. 'She will love it,' she would say on the phone, and I didn't doubt she would. I too was excited for my daughter to see it and to play with what had been my favourite toy in childhood. I wondered if watching her would be like my experience of seeing her grow up in my childhood home – if she would be drawn to the same rooms and spaces, nooks and crannies as I was. As a child I had tried to construct the doll's house as my own house in miniature. Would she want to do this too? Would she recognise the house as her house as I had done? And what changes had my mum made? Was it going to look and feel the same to me now, decades on? I realise that the new lampshades I had bought for our hall during lockdown are replicas of the one that had been in the doll's house when I was a child. Am I doing the opposite now that I am an adult, trying to make my actual home resemble my childhood doll's house in the way I had tried to make the doll's house a replica of my home when I was small? I look out of the window of my home, the house I grew up in and the one that my daughter is starting her life in too. I think of the doll's house, lights twinkling away at the other end of the Clyde, waiting expectantly for her new owner (and to see her old one again).

On bonfire night I take my cat Jimmy to the vet. Aged 21, he has been with me for the last 11 years. He was previously my ex's cat but he stayed with me when we split up. A ginger male with Maine Coon in his lineage, he was a glorious fluffy handsome boy with a gentle and docile nature. When I met my husband I told him that I thought Jimmy was on his way out, but seven years later he was still doing well. The vet visit on 5 November had been positive; the medication he had been on for his kidneys for five years was keeping him stable. For the past few years his weight had been decreasing and his ginger bulk had diminished, his body more bony underneath all of the fluff but he was bounding over the neighbour's fence and was generally still like a big kitten. He had been taken away from his mum too early and so for his whole life had liked to grip onto people's clothing with his teeth and pad away like a kitten trying to get milk. This would result in large damp patches of saliva appearing on whatever garment you were wearing. When a friend of mine visited one time, Jimmy clamped his teeth directly in between her breasts and proceeded to sook away quite happily, oblivious to the embarrassment he was causing. I often joked before I had a child that I would have my baby on one arm and Jimmy sooking away at the other side. Although I had been preparing myself for Jimmy's death due to his advanced age, it was still a shock. Two days after his check up on bonfire night, he suffered a massive stroke which paralysed his back legs and left him in excruciating pain. How do I know he was in such pain? I have never heard him make noises like he did that morning when I found him in his cat litter box, immobile from the waist down. It is almost too distressing to write about that horrible morning when, once again, we were at the vet for the worst possible reason, at the same vet and in the same room where Lola had passed away almost a year ago exactly. While Lola's death was a shock at a young 13 (compared to Jimmy's 21 years), what was harder about this time was that it was during a pandemic.

When we took him in, the same vet I had seen two days before (and who had euthanised Lola) told me there was nothing they could do. She said that my husband could join me for the procedure. I was grateful for this as I was not sure what was possible during the pandemic, but she assured me we could both be there, masked and behind a Perspex screen for his final moments. I definitely did not want my daughter there as I knew it would be too distressing, but we had no grandparents who were local enough to be there in the next half hour, and this would have been against the rules anyway. After four missed calls, we ended up managing to get hold of my aunt, who took my daughter for a walk for the time that we were with Jimmy as he passed away, another devastating morning of grief and shock. I kept trying to make myself feel grateful for all the time with him, but it was impossible not to feel the sense of bad things happening again and again, of loss and grief and pain. These moments in life are hard anyway but the pandemic on top of this makes it feel almost unbearable.

My sister and her partner came over for a socially distanced meeting in the garden in the afternoon. We were going to cancel but needed something to take our minds off what had happened. When my daughter woke up for her nap she came outside with my husband. 'Jimmy,' she called again, 'Jimmy, where are you?' I remained mute. How to tell her what has happened, how to explain mortality to a child, at a different stage this time, more cognisant, more aware? I shied away from it that day, I just couldn't, her searching round the garden for him breaking my heart just a little bit more than it was already. Becoming mother is becoming cowardly, becoming afraid of being the one who has to tell the truth about the world and the pain that is in it. Months later she still calls for him along with our other two cats – we have gone from four to two in just over a year – the cat gang are muted in colour now, monochrome, diminished, the house much quieter, the fluffy mess less. It saddens me but also heartens me in some way that she remembers him, that she still calls and hopes he will appear again one of these days. I wish he would too.

CHAPTER 14

A Covid Christmas

I WROTE OF the festive period in 2019 when my mother was in intensive care, that 'it was a Christmas like no other'. Little was I to know what the end of 2020 had in store for us. Eight hundred people tested positive in Scotland on 13 December, and my husband and I were two of them, after an outbreak in our daughter's nursery.

Upon arrival at her nursery on Thursday morning, my husband was told they would be closed. Autumn's three main carers had tested positive and we were aware of how affectionate she was with them. I had three missed calls from him and when he arrived back we stared at each other and tried to work out a complex day of meetings (for him) and final assessments and tutorials (for me). We couldn't get her to nap so she joined me for our end of year winter social on Zoom for students and staff (she sang 'Jingle Bells' as her party piece). We went into isolation as a precaution due to the outbreak in the nursery and the nursery closed from this day onwards for a number of weeks.

The next day we were so exhausted that I ordered a take-away Greggs for our lunch. After her sausage roll, we gave her a doughnut to eat while my husband was in a meeting with her. When I picked her up to take her into the kitchen she had a fine dust of sugar all over her cheeks. I licked it off. When my husband came through I told him about licking the sugar off her face. He said he had licked it all off her hands. 'I had her whole hand in my mouth,' he said. We have never licked our child before and I laughed and said, 'Why have we only started licking her in a pandemic?'

On Friday night my husband fell ill and I became ill on the Saturday. We booked a COVID-19 test for the Sunday morning at 10.00am. When we got tested, I was worried we were wasting their time as we did not have the main symptoms, a fever, cough or loss of taste and smell. It started like a bad cold but we were concerned enough about the outbreak at my daughter's nursery to book a test at the testing centre at Glasgow Airport. 2020 had a dystopian feel throughout but nothing could have prepared me for the post-apocalyptic aesthetic of Glasgow Airport's drive through COVID-19 testing facility. People in full PPE, masks and visors hold signs up saying 'DO NOT OPEN YOUR WINDOW'. Charades are performed through the glass to direct you where to go, my husband waving his phone around to indicate that we had an online booking. When he had been tested here previously, a few months before, he had administered the test himself, but this time, we are tested by the staff there – the invasive nasal and throat swabs making my eyes water. We had decided not to get our daughter tested – she had no symptoms and the government advice is that testing is only for those with symptoms but my husband had also been worried that it would be invasive and distressing for her. We drove home and waited.

She sat surrounded by bubbles. I felt warm water splash on my face and heard the sound of her laughter. We FaceTimed my parents as she played with her bath toys. Our plans for Christmas had been uncertain, we were unsure about visiting my parents unless we could self-isolate for 14 days first and this seemed impossible due to my daughter's nursery and husband's work. I had considered taking her out of nursery early, but my mum had been worried about her missing all of the Christmas activities and parties. As we had to isolate anyway due to the outbreak at her nursery, we had returned to the idea of us being able to go to visit them on the 25th – it would be as safe as it could be with our period of isolation. We were just discussing our festive plans, my mum hopeful that we might all be together after all while my daughter splashed happily in the bath, when my husband got a text on his phone. 'I'm positive,' he said. 'Oh no!' I laughed and checked my phone. 'Me too!' We were incredulous, my parents looked worried, we signed off to let the news settle. We had it. We had COVID-19. All of the horror of the news of the last year landed directly in our bathroom on a Sunday evening.

It didn't seem real and a sense of fear of what was going to happen settled on our family home. New symptoms seemed to develop every day. What started like a bad cold took a turn for the worse the first night I was ill. I awoke around 2.00am shivering violently. I had no fever (one of the most publicised symptoms) but had a sense of deep iciness within me, as though my bones themselves were cold. My body spasmed as it tried to heat itself up. I implored my husband to go and get the duvet from the bed in the spare room then he hugged me while I tried to get warm. It was a miserable night and I felt terrible the next morning, headachey and bleary. During my Monday morning meeting I could hardly concentrate, I kept forgetting what I was saying mid-sentence and found it so embarrassing I had to excuse myself to go to the toilet and cry with frustration. I have since read about some of the neurological effects of COVID-19 but at the time the headaches (swift and sudden, like a lightning bolt to the brain), the brain fog and the sense of confusion was bewildering. The second night was the same, violent shaking, frozen bones, feeling my skeleton rattle around in my skin under two heaped duvets. I felt ill in my bones and began to be short of breath.

My husband developed a cough around four days into having the virus and every day each of our symptoms evolved. Contrary to what we had heard about COVID-19, neither of us ever had a fever although we both had the intense night-shivers at different points. I did not develop a cough the whole time. My husband retained all his senses while I lost my sense of taste and smell and suffered from intense headaches, brain fog and an extremely hoarse voice, none of which he experienced. It was like we had different illnesses, and I did worry that the symptoms seemed so different to what we had heard – how many people might have it but not get tested as they did not have the symptoms most widely publicised?

Losing my sense of taste and smell was devastating. Only in the absence of these senses did I realise how integral they are to my experience of the world. The vanishing of this palate of taste and olfactory experiences felt like a grief, mind blowing. I was so relieved when they returned, although for many months afterwards things didn't smell or taste exactly as they did before I had the virus. Coffee tasted horribly burnt for the first weeks and months afterwards had a slightly unpleasant tang. The chemical buzzing in my sinuses, a plasticky, resiny sensation which was so intense in the first week, for the months afterwards also comes and goes, a reminder of the damage that has been done to some nerves and glands from having the virus.

Fear, dismay, anxiety. In the first days of having the virus it did feel quite frightening. People of all ages were becoming seriously ill and dying from it. As the symptoms evolved day by day, worsening day by day, it was hard not to worry about at what point things start to become very serious. We were not extremely ill, in that we did not need hospital treatment and were able to recover at home, but it was the most ill I have been in my adult life and the fact that we were both feeling so poorly at the same time, with no way of getting any support or childcare due to the need to self-isolate, made it harder.

Almost everyone who got the virus thought they were taking precautions. Yet many people have it. A woman posts online about how she has been shielding, not having seen a soul for all these months. She took one parcel from the postman the week before and one delivery of shopping, no physical contact, maintained social distancing, and still tested positive for the virus at the hospital. A new strain is said to be 70 per cent more transmissible than the first strain. I imagine the virus mutating, shapeshifting to spread further, wider, to infiltrate open spaces as well as indoor ones, to linger on surfaces longer, an invisible assailant. While news of the vaccines being rolled out throughout the winter months had brought palpable relief that the end of this might be in sight, the new strain seems to have diminished a lot of the hope that had been in the air.

The vaccine updates are confusing. Some types must be stored at a very low temperature and transported quickly to their destination. As thousands of lorries queue up at ports – the combined result of the decision of many European countries to shut borders with the UK to stop the new strain spreading, and the nightmarish realisation of the very weak Brexit deal which is signed off blithely by politicians on Christmas Eve – my confidence in the actual delivery of this is not high.

I read the news story of the pharmacist in Milwaukee who destroyed hundreds of doses of the vaccine at the medical centre where he worked. The intention had been to still administer the drugs so that people would think that they had been vaccinated when the drugs would not have worked. I say to my husband, surely you can't be against vaccination and mask-wearing if you are a pharmacist? He jokes, 'Maybe they know something about the vaccine that we don't.' In the UK, the vaccine is being administered in two parts. A cheery interview with 86-year-old William Shakespeare shows his glee and relief that the first batch is out. However, although the trials have been done with the second dose being administered in three weeks, suddenly the second dose can be taken up to 12 weeks after.

Inconsistencies, altering narratives; it is hard to know what to believe and feel when people's lives are at stake.

My daughter's vocabulary during our time together in the first lockdown included words with guttural sounds and hard consonants: cracker, papa, ta, Gruffalo, foot. In our second lockdown midway through December her language has evolved; she is now speaking in sentences or almost-sentences – a series of strung together thoughts or memories. I am amazed at the things she remembers, the stories she tells me. Months ago, we had dropped her Gruffalo hat when out for a walk and my aunt ran back and found it in a puddle. My daughter tells this story, again and again, in its basic form. Gruffalo hat, puddle, aunt Mo. She also has set phrases that she has learned at nursery – 'ready, steady go!' is a favourite. Others I like less: 'silly me' when she drops something (I don't really want her to think of herself as a silly girl); and 'scary monsters', which she says when she is frightened or when it is dark. I don't want her to be afraid of scary monsters but am not sure how honest to be with her about what there is to be afraid of. During the pandemic I have tried to be clear with her about what we need to do but without giving her anxiety or fear about what is happening. After all, this world of face-coverings, social distancing and seemingly inexplicable reduction of our family unit to a bubble of three at various points of the year, is all she knows. The pandemic is her normal and she is as competent at mask-wearing as she is at putting on her own jacket (her constant iteration that she would do it HERSELF).

Other favourite phrases include 'I am party ready!', a saying I used a few times when she was a baby when she was wearing a particularly snazzy outfit (but that I don't recall saying to her in the past year). She called out to me one day as she elatedly had managed to put on two (odd) sparkly shoes, gifted from our friend's child: 'I am party ready, Mummy!' On Christmas night, when I took over from bedtime after my husband had been trying to get her to sleep for over an hour, I slipped into her room wearing my black velvet dress with diamantes on it, an attempt to feel festive despite having a Covid-Christmas. She cuddled into me then stroked the soft fabric on my arm. She looked at me then leaned in for a whisper: 'You are party ready, Mummy'.

Her observations on life are simple but true. On seeing an advert on a bus-stop for coffee on one of our first post-Covid strolls round our area she informs us frankly 'Daddy loves coffee, me loves chips'. We walk around counting the Christmas trees in people's windows; we haven't been outside in so long we had forgotten about all of the lights and decorations beyond our own fairy-light-laden front room.

One of the traditions in my family has been my parents, sister and I (and more recently my daughter) making the Christmas cake every year. In late October or early November we would congregate in a kitchen, usually my mother's, to put together the alchemy of ingredients that would result in our family Christmas cake. This would be a vast volume of mixed fruit, some rustically chopped glace cherries and walnuts, chopped almonds, dark brown sugar, flour, large globs of ginger (left in big chunks, my mum loves to get a big burst of taste of each of the ingredients) and a heady mixture of cinnamon, cloves, nutmeg and dried ginger too (for good measure). Thick black spoons of treacle would bind together the concoction (only ever used at Christmas, after which my sister and I would alternately take the rest of the red and gold tin home to languish in the cupboard till the next year when a new tin would be bought regardless) and then each of us would heave the wooden spoon around the hefty batter and give it a lucky stir where we would make a wish as we bound the ingredients together. Why so many months before Christmas? So that the near-black cake that would emerge after three or four hours in the oven could sit, wrapped in two layers of greaseproof paper and two layers of tinfoil, in a darkened cupboard being brought out every fortnight to get doused in whisky. In these weeks of steeping in the dark, the plentiful fruit would grow rich and boozy, ready for its appearance at the table for Christmas dinner. It would emerge a few days before and day by day be armored with: first a layer of apricot jam mixed with boiling water to form a seal for any wayward crumbs; then a thick layer of marzipan (my cousin's favourite); then finally, on Christmas Eve, after an excruciating arm-juddering session of beating egg-whites, glycerin and icing sugar (with a dash of lemon) using my mother's hand mixer (which is around 30 years old and looks it) the final layer of royal icing, manipulated into peaks with a flourish to resemble little mounds of snow.

The recipe for the Christmas cake is a (now brown and stained) ripped-out page of a 1982 *Women's Own* magazine.

Referred to as 'the ancient parchment', for the last 15 years or so it has been kept in a plastic poly pocket to keep it from falling apart. My sister and I have taken photographs of it, should it completely disintegrate and (horror of horrors), the recipe be lost from our family. One year, my mother thought she had lost it and Christmas was very nearly ruined seven weeks before it happened. Luckily, it appeared squashed beneath the pages of the *Hamlyn All Colour Cookbook*, another of my mother's classics, and the ritual of baking the Christmas cake was able to go ahead as planned. The recipe for the royal icing was from *Mrs Beeton's Book of Household Management* – a Victorian tome which lived on the top shelf of a kitchen cupboard. My sister and I used to mimic my mother by saying 'Mrs Beeton says!' while my mum would heave the book down to consult on some recipe or another when trying to prepare for a dinner party. The ritual of making the Christmas cake, from the buying of ingredients (always the same but still worthy of discussion every year), the day of combining ingredients and lining baking tins, in a kitchen full of the smell of spices and the warm house as it baked for hours on end, allowing the essence of Christmas to permeate the entire house, its regular dousing, then the days of various layering until it was ready to be adorned with the traditional decorations. These were: a Fimo angel my sister made when she was younger (the running joke in the family being that the end of a pencil my sister had used to indent her mouth has made the angel eternally look like a blow-up doll), a lopsided Santa made by me and, if we are with my aunt's family (as we usually were), some ancient decorations from my uncle's mother, devoid of all paint but apparently once a Santa and snowman. These various oddities on top of the beautifully peaked snow of the rock-hard royal icing perhaps made for a strange looking final offering, but everyone round the table always said it looked beautiful.

In the first year of my daughter's life, only five weeks old, she was there in the kitchen, a little starfish in her Pavlik harness, held over the cake to do her (supported) good luck stir before falling asleep on her papa's fleece for the remainder of the proceedings. The next year, at one year old, she was more animated, enjoying the stir, bopping about in my kitchen with my parents and my sister. My mum shrieked that she was going to get the mixture everywhere and we all laughed. I have it on video. I am holding her, she wears a red festive dress and I have on my Christmas jumper for the occasion. We are happy and laughing, we are together. You can't tell from the video, but the kitchen smells enticing and we all retire to the living room for a glass of wine while the oven does its magic in turning the brown gloop speckled with a million raisins and orange bits into the magical cake we all love.

In the run up to Christmas 2020, we talk in sombre tones about what will happen to the Christmas cake this year. My parents buy the ingredients alone and my mum says she will make it herself in her kitchen. I ask her to FaceTime us and think that maybe we will bake along, together but remote, continuing the ritual at a distance. On the Saturday she makes it herself, sending a blurry picture of my dad's lucky stir. We are not together, we can't be, and the ritual of decades is broken. The cake is baked.

I don't smell it and no-one apart from my parents had their lucky stirs. I am bereft. As Christmas together seems less and less likely, my mum sticks the cake in the freezer for a time when we can be together again. Once we get Covid, it is joined by the turkey and the pigs in blankets, waiting patiently until the pandemic is over and we can defrost Christmas. We did it last year due to mum's surgery and had Christmas 2019 in February 2020. When will we be able to have Christmas 2020?

CHAPTER 15

Phase Three

AS THE END of the year approached cases spiked in the UK to over 55,000 positive tests in one day, more than 2,000 of these being in Scotland. The new strain of the virus was throwing previous contingencies and arrangements out of the window. An image was circulated on social media of the Live Aid concert in 1985. It shows Wembley Stadium, packed with nearly 80,000 people. This is how many have died of COVID-19 in the UK to date. It is a sobering image. As the death toll has risen exponentially, it has almost become abstracted, unreal. If this number of people were killed in any other way it would be a scandal, an outrage. As predicted, the UK has the highest death toll in Europe and it is hard not to question how this could have been allowed to happen. There are still no quarantine arrangements for travel, people continue to enter the UK from other places without isolating, as they have been for almost a year. Things could have been so different, so much better. Instead, as the new year approaches, the numbers of cases and death toll are only getting worse. I avoided getting involved in conversations on social media about how 2021 had to be better, how 2020 had been as bad as it could possibly be. I didn't want to tempt fate but I was quietly optimistic about the new year. A few days into 2021, it is clear that things are getting worse.

A week into the new year, the world has witnessed a storming of The Capitol in the US, a performance of white privilege and the erosion of democracy and law as men, white men (many of them we later learn who are police officers themselves), parade the stately rooms with confederate flags. 2021 America seems like 2020 America but with less of a handle on democracy, with Trump still clinging on to power and to hell with what the people want. Americans are angry, with by far the highest global number of cases and overall deaths in the world, a healthcare system that is not accessible for all and where having wealth affects your access to care. The situation is becoming unhinged. Global cases exceed one million and the virus shows no signs of abating, with new strains emerging that are even more transmissible. The South African variant that emerged in the UK prior to Christmas dampened the hope that the roll out of the vaccine had promised.

On the first lockdown, in April 2020, Captain Tom Moore, the pensioner who had aimed to walk 100 lengths of his garden to raise £1,000 for charity before his 100th birthday ended up becoming a national hero after raising over £30 million pounds for the NHS. He was launched into the spotlight and became symbolic of every person doing their bit for the greater good (although why a retired captain should be trying to support the underfunded NHS is a question for the government). His death on 2 February 2021, from pneumonia then COVID-19, seemed like a cruel irony, a sad end to an inspirational story of how he found fame in his 100th year.

This third lockdown is harder, colder, meaner than the previous ones. Part of this is due to the fact it is winter, the days darker and greyer, the weather too cold to spend much time outside. For days on end in January the rain lashes the windows, sideways slanting rain, visible in its fervor under streetlights through the night and speckling the windowpanes during the day. Our arts and crafts box is out constantly as I try to find new things to stimulate my daughter, new things to engage her with, but I can tell that she too is fed up of this new phase and bored of only having us to play with.

Since we caught coronavirus in mid-December, our contact with others was non-existent and then became gradually minimal. A walk with my sister in the park (although it is too cold to stay out for long), a dodder down the road to see my aunt over her gate. At the weekends our ambitions are set low, even getting my daughter's coat on and making it to the end of the street before dinner time for some fresh air is about all we can manage.

In January I don't feel good. I feel slow and tired all the time. I have put on a stone in the last year and I feel sluggish and bloated. The temptation of sweet things I have baked with my daughter and a ritual glass of wine in the evening have become my only vices, but I have begun to depend on them as part of the day, of how the sameness of the days moves into night. Someone I haven't seen for a while asks me if I am pregnant again. I am not, I am hibernating, comforting myself, growing an extra layer of thick skin to try to weather these winter months, these hard times. I continue to have some lingering after-effects from Covid – most notably a disconcerting change to my senses of taste and smell, a nasty, burnt, chemically residue seems to permeate my sinuses.

The other symptom that persists is headaches. Brain-freezing, terrifying headaches. Like a lightning bolt to the brain or like a slow swelling throb that builds to a white-dotted crescendo, either way, they become debilitating. I become frightened of them, on the mornings that they are there, even before waking, at 5.00am I can already feel the drumming, thrumming horror of it building. Or mid-morning, while squinting at my screen, the sharp pain behind my eyes, in my temples. I have suffered from headaches throughout my adult life, but these feel more sinister, an attacking force that make my days feel unmanageable. Then there is the fatigue. It is hard to know if this is an ongoing symptom of Covid or if it is a symptom of living through a pandemic, almost a year in with hardly any childcare or respite to the relentless onslaught of the days.

There is some surprising good news. My parents phone on a Saturday in early February to tell us that they received the vaccine. They had received an email a few weeks before inviting them to an appointment which had turned out to be a scam. The email had made mention about 'recent procedures and family history', perhaps an easy assumption for many people to read as specific to them, but on phoning the doctors and NHS were told it was not real and most likely a scam. To try to get pensioners, eager for the vaccine, to give details online in order to defraud them seems so low.

When they do get the call to get the vaccine, it is quick and efficient. My aunt gets hers on the same day at the Louisa Jordan hospital (housed in the Scottish Exhibition and Conference Centre near the Clyde) and says it was all run with military efficiency. My cousins are getting theirs, my friends' parents too. Relief, that this first dose has been administered. Despite having had the virus, my Covid anxiety since the start of the year (of inadvertently passing it on to someone), has been through the roof. The doctor I see about my recurring headaches says they don't know enough about it yet to be able to say with certainty that people who have had the virus are immune – there have been many cases of reinfection.

At the start of February it snows. When there had been a day of snow in January I had not been able to get my daughter dressed in the morning to make it outside. I hated myself for missing that day of snow, chastising myself for letting her miss out on that experience due to the chaos of the days. This time, I was determined that we were going to make the most of it. When a few white flakes fluttered down at teatime I checked the forecast and saw that snow was expected to fall overnight. When we awoke the next morning the world was transformed. She and I were up early, in the dark, peering out the window to the ghostly white world. 'It's snowman day!' she shrieked to her daddy to wake him up and we were out the front door into the gentle blizzard before nine o'clock. It was almost too powdery and fresh to build with but my husband lay down and made a snow angel in the road and my daughter's cheeks became rosy in the cold. It was so deep her wellies were becoming submerged in it, with some of the drift falling into her boots. She was entranced but after a while said, 'It's cold, Mummy,' so, after building a mini snowman on the bench, with her dolly's hat and a ribbon for a scarf, two stones that made it look like it was wearing sunglasses, we retreated inside.

We were out again later, this time with a bucket to build a bigger snowman. The neighbours had been using a crate and a saw to make bricks for an impressive igloo, within which was a chunky snowman. Our second snowman, decked with a cap and scarf, sat in the middle of the path, gazing cheerily back at anybody that looked in the gate. Our neighbours lent us a sled so we did not have to sit my daughter in the tray from the kitchen I had looked out as a substitute. Her face broke into a wide beam as she began hurtling down the hill. 'I like it,' she said, 'I like fast!' These snow days felt different, the white covering over the streets, trees and houses had temporarily transformed the world. Families wearing bright coloured winter jackets dragging red and blue sledges behind them filled the streets. People were outside for the first time in ages to enjoy this winter wonderland. Snowballs were thrown and there was the jovial noise of people laughing, strangers smiling at each other in the street as they braved the snow and trailed the sledges to the top of the hill. Bobble hats and rosy cheeks and a feeling of lightness, of this being a holiday, an escape from the monotony of the lockdown days, all blurring into each other. These snow days were different, some respite from the insides of our houses, a way to be outside together and to see the world anew.

I always thought she would be a water baby. I love the water and imagined that we would spend a lot of time at the swimming baths, or swimming in the sea on family holidays. By the age of two she has only been in the water a handful of times. In the early months we could not take her swimming because of her Pavlik harness (a bath at home was out of the question, never mind immersion in a public pool). After this was removed, the swimming baths did not regularly make it into our schedule of baby classes – I wanted my husband there with me to help navigating a slippery baby in and out of the pool. When I was back at work it became hard to fit everything we wanted to do into a weekend, and then, when the pandemic hit, all public pools were closed and when they briefly reopened in the summer I was reluctant to go as I was nervous about the virus. We did swim in the sea and in a pool when we went on holiday in August 2020 which was a blissful week of sun and relaxation, but since then she has remained a terrestrial being, no more aquatic adventures have been possible as we moved deeper into lockdown over the winter months.

When I ask her if her food is too hot she says insistently, 'It's fine!' When we look out the window and it is raining and I ask if we should postpone our walk she claims, 'It's fine!' I wonder if my overly positive attitude and persistence that everything is okay (when clearly it is not) is rubbing off on her. I think this until I see her solemnly reporting into the plastic microphone on her toy till as though she is asking for a clean-up on aisle three, 'Mummy's sad'. She is becoming more perceptive as she develops, and with this, her understanding of what is actually happening seems to also be coming into sharper focus. She still calls for our cat Jimmy who passed away in November. She doesn't call for Lola, but she remembers her and points to her picture on the fridge sometimes. She notices things, understands things and I begin to have to carefully choose my words when speaking to her about why we are doing the things we are doing.

Almost a year into lockdown I notice that the walls in the bathroom are starting to crack again. In the first months of the pandemic I had applied Polyfilla to the deep fractures gouging the bathroom walls up towards the ceiling. I had scraped the white paste into the schisms and then painted over them in white emulsion. Because of the angles in the bathroom I never felt as though it was immaculate but overall I was pleased with the job and the coats of white paint and lack of visible cracks had made me realise just now dingy it was before.

The cracks are back, and the white now seems off-colour, grey-ish at points and I wonder what is causing these fractures in the wall I had repaired. What is lurking beneath the walls trying to make itself known? Is my home to be like the Forth Road Bridge? The structure which famously needs the start of it repainted as soon as the mammoth task of painting it is complete? My mother's father had worked as a welder and had told me stories of the famous red bridge. What was fixed then needs redone now. It has been a year since I did it, the blink of an eye and a lifetime.

My daughter pinches the skin on the back of my hand and I have a flashback to a conversation with my mother, many years ago. She was in recovery from her cancer and we were sitting at the kitchen table. I remember her touching the skin on the back of my hand and commenting on how soft it was, how youthful. I had never really noticed this before but to demonstrate the contrast with hers, she pinched the skin on the back of her hand. When she gripped the skin with the blue and purple veins a trace under the surface, it lifted up with the pressure from the gesture. It was so malleable that it stayed for a moment, poised in the raised position she had stretched it to, before slowly melting back into the surface of her hand. She did the same gesture to me and my skin pinged back, immediately returning to its place. As I stand outdoors with my daughter, almost a year into lockdown, she does the same action to me, pinching and slightly twisting the skin on the back of my hand. I see my own papery skin now as my mother's was then, leisurely returning to its rightful place. I am nearly 40; what age was she when we shared this moment? Just over 50? Once again the years collapse into each other. I am her, my daughter is me, the same action repeated, a different time, and a different perspective. I was young, I am older. My mum was old to me then, older now. My daughter just at the start, living these actions over again.

I lie in her cot with her trying to comfort her to go to sleep. 'Do you want a song?' I ask. 'Yeah'. I start to softly sing 'Go to Sleep My Baby,' gently stroking her back as I do so. 'No!' she says, 'that's a Granny song'. I begin the opening line to 'Papa's Gonna Buy You a Mockingbird'. 'No! That's a Granny song'. 'You are My Sunshine'. 'No!' she says, in an exasperated voice.

'That's a GRANNY song.' I pause and then tell her that all of Mummy's songs are Granny songs because they are the songs that Granny used to sing to Mummy when she was a wee girl. She thinks about this for a moment. 'I am a wee girl,' she says. 'Mummy not a wee girl'. 'But I was,' I explain to her, 'and Granny used to sing these songs to me too'.

Parenting in a pandemic has exposed the precarious nature of it all. Work-life balance was never particularly successful in the before-times, but now every day teeters on the brink of pandemonium. Although the day-to-day experience of working and doing full-time childcare was challenging, our precarity was not as extreme as many others. Our jobs were secure, we were not feeling the angst of unemployment, furlough, bereavement or, since the start of the year, illness. We were in a privileged position and have been continually grateful for this. Why then did this lockdown seem so much harder than the first? Perhaps it is that the novelty has worn off, maybe it is the accumulative effect of a year in some kind of isolation. Since the start of 2021 the winter has seemed harsher, the days short and brutish, the air seemingly filled with a sense of threat as well as that of contagion. We are missing connection. We are missing seeing family and friends and being able to make choices without worrying about the ethical implications around other people's health. We are feeling the responsibility of our choices. Let me speak for myself, I am feeling the responsibility of my choices. I am exhausted from the constant anxiety around the virus. I am missing having things to look forward to a year into this limbo existence.

CHAPTER 16

Explaining the Inexplicable

ON THE EVE of my 38th birthday a woman went missing after walking home from a friend's house near Clapham Common in London. A few days later, on the day my mother's two sisters have their birthdays, a man was arrested on suspicion of kidnap. A few days after that he was arrested for her murder. He was an active member of the Metropolitan Police with the Parliamentary and Diplomatic Protection Unit. Sarah Everard was born in the same year as my sister. Her remains were found on 10 March in a builder's bag in Hoad's Wood in Ashford, Kent. On 16 March, the day of my sister's wedding anniversary (and also of my mother's mother's birthday) police continued to search the area and specialist divers searched underwater for her belongings. I will not name the 48-year-old serving policeman who was arrested for her murder. I will name Sarah Everard, and I have mapped this short timeline from her disappearance to her body being found to experiences and markers in time for women in my own family. I have done this because all women have experienced violence, abuse or harassment because of their gender which means that every woman in my family will have also experienced some form of this. A study that came out on the day that Sarah Everard's body was found indicated that 97 per cent of women had been sexually harassed in public spaces. I want to acknowledge that the epidemic of violence against women has ended Sarah Everard's life, she will have no more birthdays or weddings, only a funeral. There will be no further markers in Sarah's life, only the mark that her death will leave on her family and loved ones.

On the day before Valentine's Day 2020 it was announced that the number of women killed by a partner or ex has risen by almost a third. A year of lockdown has further exacerbated these figures as women suffering domestic abuse have no respite from their abusers and the incidents of violence against women have risen sharply. It is reported that due to having to hold court cases online, some women are in the same space as their abusers while testifying. That the male that is inflicting the violence against women could be sitting in the same room, invisible to those on the screen has meant that lockdown has removed some of the only safe spaces women had. If you must 'stay at home' but your home is not safe, what then?

Rebecca Solnit addresses violence against women in *The Longest War,* a recognition that we are experiencing an unacknowledged epidemic of harm to women by men. To live with the threat of harassment is one of the experiences of being a woman that can be considered universal. It is so common and so systemic that it has become invisible. The realisation (at an increasingly young age) that your gender endangers you, that spaces are not safe, that streets should not be walked at night and that men will try to speak to you when you don't want them to, will follow you, will find out things about you and will threaten you if you spurn their advances. The understanding that men feel they have the right to touch you uninvited, to shout things about your body in public spaces, to force themselves on you and to make you hate your own body for having the things they refer to – breasts, legs, bum.

The reporting of the statistics of the numbers of women who have experienced harassment in the weeks that followed Sarah Everard's disappearance were met with shock and dismay by the press. When I say the press, I mean the largely male journalistic voices which dominate. They were surprised and horrified by this revelation. Women were not shocked by this, and I, for one, was sombre in acknowledging that my own experiences were not isolated, but instead a shared one between millions of women. The pandemic has been a strangely universalising experience – everyone in the world has been experiencing the COVID-19 pandemic in one way or another. This kind of gendered sexual harassment is a similarly universal experience for women – almost all of whom have encountered this and have experienced the threat of male sexualisation and violence.

When instances of sexual harassment began to happen to me from my teens onwards, once the fear had diminished, I would feel the most powerful outrage. What right do you have to touch me/talk to me/abuse me? What makes you think you can move through the world with this power? What makes you think that I am less of a person than you, or perhaps, in your eyes, not even a person, just a sexualised thing to be pawed or sleazed at? The answer to these questions is:

patriarchy, a system which demands the oppression of women and which has allowed many men to breeze through the world believing that they can do what they want. Particularly for men in power, the idea that 'you can take what you want' has meant that women are always there for the taking, always at risk, always vulnerable.

The outrage I would feel when I experienced unwanted male attention (to be clear, it was never wanted, I just wanted to be able to be invisible, for my body to disappear) would metamorphose to a strong, pervading and long-lasting feeling of shame. This shame would take the form of disgust at my own body for having womanly dimensions. Hatred of my inability to respond in a way that I felt was appropriate – if I challenged this behaviour, which I did more and more as I got older, another onslaught would happen as retribution, this time it might not be about my appearance, but about what I have said. When spurning advances the tables would switch in an instant – I would be told I was attractive and then when I made it clear I was not interested was immediately transformed into someone completely undesirable, the male voice raised to publicly shame me in front of others. I would go over these instances again and again in my head to try to rewrite a different response, find a different way I could have engaged with this – a way that I would have felt happy with and proud of. Of course, there is no way that I could ever feel happy with my response because it is an impossible situation. It was not my responses, but the instances themselves that were the problem. But they would still happen. To me and, as is now coming to light, to every other woman.

I also know that even in the worst situations I have been in, there have been many women much worse off, women who have suffered rape, assault, and who have lost their lives. Many have endured more than I have, but why are all women suffering? Why are any women suffering?

My daughter is two and a half when Sarah Everard is murdered. How do I speak to her about these things? How do I make her understand the threat she is under simply because of her gender? My outrage bubbles up again at the thought that I even have to find a way of preparing her for what will inevitably happen to her as she grows up, of the sexual harassment, abuse and attention that she will receive. I know however I do it I will find it inadequate, but again, it is not my response to this that will be at fault, it is the impossible circumstance of having to explain it to her in the first place. What do I say? That men hurt women? That men think they can say what they want to you? That a women's body is public property? I already know that I can't find a way of saying any of this that is going to make it okay, because it is not.

I was a woman before my mum told me of her experiences, of perverts on public transport, my mild surprise at the time that it had been going on since the 1950s. It has been going on longer than that. When will it end?

CHAPTER 17

Emerging

THE ANNIVERSARY OF the first lockdown took place on 23 March 2021. There was a minute of silence at noon to commemorate those who had died of the virus over the past year. The official death toll for the UK on this anniversary was 126,284 with 112 deaths being recorded on the day itself.

At the time of writing, there have been three phases of lockdown. The first was from 23 March 2020 to early July 2020. Then, some blissful summer months of sunshine and respite from most of the strictest measures. From September onwards there was a second phase of lockdown, but this time with some vital services (including schools and nurseries) staying open. The third lockdown began at midnight on Christmas Day, and from a minute into Boxing Day until the 22 February 2021, there was another full lockdown with complete closure (including education and all non-vital shops) as the virus cases and the death toll seemed to peak at the start of 2021. After late February some measures eased and nurseries and some school pupils were able to attend in-person again. On 4 April 2021 hairdressers and garden centres were allowed to open. The phased move out of lockdown commenced on

26 April with hospitality opening and tourism resuming in the next few months as well. Being able to go into people's houses again was possible with many areas moving into level two in May and June and the vaccine programme being successfully rolled out to vulnerable groups and other adults with Scotland moving 'beyond level 0' in August. There is a lot to be hopeful about for these coming months.

Recent reports indicate that future governmental responses will be to treat COVID-19 like a seasonal flu. Now that there is a vaccine programme, this seems possible, where before there had seemed no other way of keeping people safe apart from isolation, lockdown and increased sanitation and hygiene measures. There is a lot of debate about vaccine passports and paperwork that would make international travel, festivals and large gatherings such as sporting events possible. I have read a lot about the case against lockdowns, and the arguments which say they are ineffective. I do not know enough about the science of this to say what is right, but I do believe the statistics that indicate that earlier lockdowns and swifter action could have saved more lives. That the UK has the highest death toll in Europe (and at one point in the summer had double the amount of cases than the rest of Europe combined) seems both obscene and avoidable as we had so much more time and information than other countries and could have been more prepared. The development of new variants has meant that the containment and management of the virus is not certain, and many of the new strands (such as the Delta variant) are highly transmissible.

What has the last year meant for us? As a global community, there has been a huge sense of collective grief at the immense loss of life, more than four million people across the world dead due to COVID-19. In amongst this devastation and heartache there has been a sense that what seemed impossible might be possible, that there might be an opportunity for significant societal change. There is hope that some of the important action taken in the last year over anti-Black racism marks a paradigm shift in terms of anti-racist action and education. Despite widespread isolation, there has been solidarity, collective action and communities of people finding ways to protest, gather and challenge the status quos that have been brought into question during this year of crises. There is hope that the lack of pollution from air travel might provoke more long-lasting change around air travel and climate change. Perhaps the questions about our lives, lifestyles and priorities, provoked by the pandemic, will instigate a deeper reflection on what we are doing and how we are choosing to live our lives on a damaged planet.

For our young people, it has been a strange year of isolation and intimacy. My daughter has spent more than half of her life in this pandemic. She has had to make sense of periods of time where our bubble has reduced to the three of us, apparently inexplicably, for months on end. In the first lockdown she did not seem at all fazed by this, but by the third one she was less content for her social circle to be reduced in this way. In March 2020 she was happy to spend time with her dad and me, at home, day after day, she loved it. In the early stages of

2021, she needed more from us and from her life and couldn't understand the return to our isolated existence, this time without the fun, outdoor play that the good weather the spring the year before had afforded. She has been apart from grandparents, aunties and uncles, cousins and her friends. She is young, but she has missed them in her own way and we don't know what this means for her in the longer term. Beyond us, most of her familial contact has been through a screen – I had been so against her interacting with devices prior to the pandemic but this has been one of the survival tactics, one of the means of communicating and entertaining her that have been vital during the lockdowns while working full time.

For us, as parents in a pandemic, it has been an impossible juggle at times, both work and caring for a child are full-time endeavours and never before has the expectation of doing both simultaneously reared its head before. I feel proud that we have managed it and shameful that she has not had all of our attention during this time. I have tried to make my peace with the reality of it, of trying to ensure the day is full of enriching activities, while knowing she will need to be on the iPad at certain times. We have done our best, but it is hard to feel that it has been good enough. When my daughter returned to nursery in February 2021, I realised that at least when she was home during lockdowns, I had to step away from my screen during the working day to spend time with her. Without these windows of time to go outside or play with her for a while, the hours of headache-inducing screen time took over entire days and evenings. I would get up at 5.30am to work before she woke up, give her breakfast and see her off to nursery, work all day, give her dinner then work while she watched TV before bed, then work when she was asleep until after midnight some nights. It felt and was relentless. While the work got done and my daughter was happy to be back with her nursery friends, the toll was taken on any time my husband and I might have had for ourselves, or with each other. Over a year on and as working parents, we are still in survival mode, still trying to get through a day at a time, trying to make it to each weekend as an oasis of time without meetings scheduled. We need time to recover from this, to take a breath, to remember who we are as people and as a couple, when so many things that were vital to our perceptions of these things have been stripped away over the last year.

What has the pandemic meant for me as a mother, as a person? I have been a terrible friend in the past year, a semblance of a sister, a distracted daughter, a guilty mother and an absent wife. I have not had time for many of the things I enjoy doing, and in not doing these things, have lost some of them. As we move out of lockdown, I want to try to retain some of the reflections that emerged in the first phase that I feel have slipped away from me in the accumulative exhaustion of the pandemic. I want to live a simpler life. I want time with my daughter and my husband. I want to feel close to my parents and sister. I want to be home and enjoy my home. I want to make time to speak with old friends; they have been with me my whole life, I can't lose them now. I want to have more balance, to work less, be with my family more. I want to spend time outside every day. I want to be present, to be able to focus on the thing I am doing rather than trying to always be doing lots of things at once. I want to re-learn how to relax, to find a way of shifting gear from emergency mode, survival mode. I want to be able to do things that take time. I want to be able to read and write for pleasure. I want to be able to see my family, properly, for more than an hour. I want to be able to feel my face relax, for the tense feeling I have had in my forehead for months to release. I want to cook meals for my sister again, to serve her food at my dining room table. I want to be able to hug my mum and dad. I want to have three generations of women in my family in one room again. I want to remember the legacy of women in my family. I want to speak to my mother and daughter about our lives, about what they mean to me. I want to feel carefree again. I want to remember how lucky we have been. I don't want things to go back to normal; I want something different to emerge. I want the impetus for wider societal change that the pandemic has evoked to grow. I want the pandemic to mark a significant change in how we think about our global community, our planet and the crises it is facing. I want to remember the time with my daughter during the pandemic for what it was, a gift. She calls me Mum now, her language has developed, the sounds of her words finally formed. For my daughter and I, I want us to have time to know each other, time to be close. I want us to have time to explore together, to find things out, to notice things.

Bubbles, I think. I want us to have time for bubbles.

Acknowledgements

I WANT TO thank my family for their encouragement in writing this book. There are many people in my life who have supported my husband and me in being working parents: my parents Bob and Carolyn and sister Sarah, my in-laws Jim, Janice, Jennifer, Matt (along with our nieces Charley and Maddie). My aunt Mo, friends and colleagues have also been a source of assistance, childcare and advice, and although babysitting was not possible during the pandemic, we very much relied on our network at a distance to get through the lockdown months. My dear friend Scarlet has been with me throughout from afar.

This is my own account of my experiences as a mother and, as isolating as the lockdowns have been, my story does touch on that of many others so I am grateful to those who have given me permission to include them in this book. Thank you to Luath for publishing this work and to Gavin MacDougall in particular for his advice and for supporting new writers as well as Lauren McFarlane for her time and care in editing the manuscript, and Eilidh MacLennan, Rachael Murray and Lauren Grieve for their support with the book.

I want to thank my husband Callum and sister Sarah for their editorial support and for offering their feedback at various stages of writing. Thank you Callum for weathering this storm as our bubble of three, your love and encouragement has been invaluable. To my sister, Sarah, your kind words and gifts of bread have been so appreciated, you are an amazing auntie and sister. For you to be becoming mother during the final stages of this book, and for you and Adam to welcome your own daughter Hazel into our family, has been such a joy. Thank you to my father, Bob, for all you have done for me throughout my life and for creating my daughter's special garden.

Thank you to my mother, Carolyn, for all your care and love as a mother, and to my daughter Autumn, whose arrival into the world was the impetus for writing this book. You are teaching me how to be a mother every day and I am so grateful to have you as my daughter.

References

Baker, Peter C, 'How will the world emerge from the coronavirus crisis?' in *The Guardian*, 2020.

Bourgeois, L, '*Maman*', Guggenheim Museum Bilbao, 1999.

Braidotti, R, *Nomadic Subjects*, Columbia University Press, New York, 2011.

Cusk, R, *A Life's Work: On Becoming A Mother*, Fourth Estate, London, 2001.

Ettinger, B, *The Matrixial Borderspace*, University of Minnesota Press, Minneapolis, 2006.

Freud, S. *The Uncanny*, Penguin Modern Classics, London, 2003.

Hoare, P, 'Fatal attraction – writers' and artists' obsession with the sea' in *The Guardian*, 2017.

Jenkins, A, *Morning: How to make time: A manifesto*, HarperCollins UK, London, 2018.

Klein, N, *This Changes Everything*, Simon & Schuster, New York, 2014.

Knausgaard, K Ove, *Autumn*, Harvill Secker, London, 2017.

Mann, J, *SuperBaby: 12 Ways to Give Your Child a Head Start in the First 3 Years*, Sterling, New York, 2011.

McLaughlin, M, 'Coronavirus in Scotland: Nicola Sturgeon defends building ban' in *The Times*, 2020.

Moore, J, 'The scenes on Bournemouth beach make Britain look like the jackass of the world' in *The Independent*, 2020.

Morton, T, *Being Ecological*, Penguin UK, London, 2018.

Nelson, M, *The Argonauts*, Melville House UK, London, 2016.

Rich, A, *Of Woman Born: Motherhood as Experience and Institution*, WW Norton and Company, New York, 1976.

Silva, C, 'Parties – Not Protests – Are Causing Spikes In Coronavirus' in *National Public Radio*, 2020.

Solnit, R, *The Faraway Nearby*, Granta Books, London, 2013.

Solnit, R, "The impossible has already happened': what coronavirus can teach us about hope' in *The Guardian,* 2020.

Solnit, R, 'The Longest War' in *Men Explain Things to Me*, Haymarket Books, Chicago, 2014.

Tsing, A, *The Mushroom at the End of the World*, Princeton University Press, Princeton, 2015.

Luath Press Limited

committed to publishing well written books worth reading

LUATH PRESS takes its name from Robert Burns, whose little collie Luath (*Gael.*, swift or nimble) tripped up Jean Armour at a wedding and gave him the chance to speak to the woman who was to be his wife and the abiding love of his life. Burns called one of the 'Twa Dogs' Luath after Cuchullin's hunting dog in Ossian's *Fingal*. Luath Press was established in 1981 in the heart of Burns country, and is now based a few steps up the road from Burns' first lodgings on Edinburgh's Royal Mile. Luath offers you distinctive writing with a hint of unexpected pleasures.

Most bookshops in the UK, the US, Canada, Australia, New Zealand and parts of Europe, either carry our books in stock or can order them for you. To order direct from us, please send a £sterling cheque, postal order, international money order or your credit card details (number, address of cardholder and expiry date) to us at the address below. Please add post and packing as follows: UK – £1.00 per delivery address; overseas surface mail – £2.50 per delivery address; overseas airmail – £3.50 for the first book to each delivery address, plus £1.00 for each additional book by airmail to the same address. If your order is a gift, we will happily enclose your card or message at no extra charge.

Luath Press Limited
543/2 Castlehill
The Royal Mile
Edinburgh EH1 2ND
Scotland
Telephone: +44 (0)131 225 4326 (24 hours)
Email: sales@luath.co.uk
Website: www.luath.co.uk